COME UP HIGHER!

REDISCOVERING THRONE LIFE— THE HIGHEST CHRISTIAN LIFE FOR THE 21ST CENTURY

A Classic and Contemporary Treasury
of the Higher Life

BY PAUL L. KING

TIMOTHY
Publishing Services

Published by Timothy Publishing Services
3409 W Gary St
Broken Arrow, OK 74012
918-924-6246

ISBN-13: 978-1-940931-04-3

Library of Congress catalog card number: 2013954717

Printed in the United States of America

ENDORSEMENTS

"I have always been amazed by the paradox presented in Scripture: the humble are exalted; the hungry are full; the yielded are powerful; and those who go deeper live a higher life. In *Come Up Higher*, Dr. Paul King has masterfully brought together influential voices from church history who have experienced and written about the higher life in Christ—the Throne Life. Their voices instruct, illustrate, and challenge us to live in the heavenlies, with Christ. Any Christian who desires to see the empowerment of life in Christ influence his or her walk, worship, or spiritual warfare will find this powerful collection of insights from 2,000 years of church history indispensable."

—Dr. Gary Benedict, President,
The Christian and Missionary Alliance

"*Come Up Higher* is a great book! It is greatly needed in today's church to bring correction to the extremes of not having courageous faith, not walking in authority or power on the one hand; and the other extreme of attempting to walk in the authority of imputed righteousness, moving in power, exercising faith, without the holiness of imparted righteousness. Dr. Paul King's book, *Come Up Higher! Rediscovering Throne Life—The Highest Christian Life for the 21st Century*, is a well written, powerful book bringing balance to a subject where balance has often not been found. I highly recommend it."

—Randy Clark, Founder and President of
Global Awakening and the Apostolic
Network of Global Awakening

"*Come Up Higher! Rediscovering Throne Life—The Highest Christian Life for the 21st Century* is another life-changing book from Paul King. He brings us to the pinnacle of the Christian life with a privilege that is almost unimaginable and is the clearest expression of *heaven on earth* possible. It is about position and Presence.

With great wisdom, Paul deals with both the obstacles and the overwhelming benefits of this lifestyle. I can't imagine reading this book without increasing in hunger for a lifestyle that is almost too good to be true. This is the book that will drive a person into the *secret place* without striving or religious agendas."

—Bill Johnson, Author, *When Heaven Invades Earth* and *Hosting the Presence* Bethel Church, Redding, CA

CONTENTS

Dedication

To the church planting congregation of Higher Life Fellowship,

Broken Arrow, Oklahoma

Who have shared together with me

In spreading and living out the message

Of the Higher Christian Life.

Acknowledgements

Thanks and appreciation to the people who have stirred me higher in Christ, so many that I can name only a few. Dr. James Barber, friend and professor of Practical Ministry at Oral Roberts University, and Dr. Tim McKitrick, another friend, colleague and prayer partner, have stirred me to publish this work. Darlene Kipling has been a mother in the faith and mentor to me in the Higher Life. My wife Kathy journeys with me in the Higher Life. Sam Barsoum, who was my worship pastor for three years, and his wife Liz, have carried us higher into the Holy of Holies in worship. When diagnosed with cancer in 2007, a retired pastor friend, Paul Hull, encouraged me to look down upon my circumstances from my position on the Throne in the heavenly places.

My father John King stirred my interest in the writings of A.W. Tozer, having sat under Tozer's ministry. My pastors growing up led me into the Higher Life teachings of A.B. Simpson. My aunt Lois King, missionary to Africa, introduced me to the Higher Life writings of Andrew Murray. My mentors through the years have challenged me to press on.

Dr. Gary Benedict, President of The Christian and Missionary Alliance, has encouraged me to share the message of the Higher Christian Life, and has given me a platform to present within the Alliance. Dr. Bill Randall, pastor of Risen King Community Church, Redding, California, and Dr. Ron Walborn, Dean of Alliance

Theological Seminary, Nyack, New York, have shared together kinship with me in promoting the Higher Life vision.

Also, special thanks go to Becky Duncan, Rhonda Sandberg, and Connie Vugteveen, members of my congregation who helped to edit the book, as well as to cheer me on to share the Higher Life message.

Kathryn Kuhlman once spurred me on with her words, "It is great to be baptized in the Spirit, *but there is so much more.*" Dr. Neil T. Anderson, founder of Freedom in Christ Ministries, has encouraged me to write on our identity in Christ and our authority as a believer. Joe McIntyre introduced me to George Peck, who wrote the original book on Throne Life. Bill Johnson and Randy Clark have inspired me with their message, "There is more!" And so, I press on!

Foreword

by Bill Johnson

When the apostle Paul spoke of our being "seated in heavenly places," he wasn't merely giving us an inspirational thought to turn to when we face a difficulty or a confession to make to illustrate our faith. This vital revelation from Scripture is much more than a doctrinal statement. It is an invitation to an encounter . . . a lifestyle . . . a divine perspective on reality. In it we are summoned to enter a lifestyle only dreamt of by the prophets of old. And it's available to every believer. Throughout history many have called this the *Throne Life*.

Come Up Higher! Rediscovering Throne Life—The Highest Christian Life for the 21st Century is another life-changing book from Paul King. And I can't think of a more significant subject for him to write about. He brings us to the pinnacle of the Christian life with a privilege that is almost unimaginable and is the clearest expression of *heaven on earth* possible. It is about position and Presence.

The throne is the center of a kingdom. The throne room of God is the place of greatest glory and presence and is the ultimate reality—the place of our greatest significance. With great wisdom, Paul deals with both the obstacles and the overwhelming benefits of this lifestyle. I can't imagine reading this book without increasing in hunger for a lifestyle that is almost too good to be true. This is the book that will drive a person into the *secret place* without striving or religious agendas. Instead of the pressure to pray to be more spiritual, the heart thrills with the realization and conviction, "I've been invited!" This brings a confidence that is entirely born out of grace instead of entitlement. It is brilliant.

Paul King's scholarship benefits the reader in so many ways. His writing is thorough without being sterile. The reader benefits not only from Paul's insights and experiences, but also from the writings of the giants of faith throughout history. Paul is one of the most well-read individuals I've ever met. He has done the research for us, gleaning from the priceless writings of another era, giving us a sense of *divine momentum* that most of us are unaware of. His ability to draw from history and put their words and experiences into a 21st century setting is extraordinary.

I especially love how practical he has made a subject that easily becomes so mystical. With great wisdom and grace, he shows how this throne life affects every part of the human experience, from health and resources, to the vital aspects of personal holiness.

—Bill Johnson
Author, *When Heaven Invades Earth* and
Hosting the Presence
Bethel Church, Redding, CA

Foreword

by Randy Clark

Paul King's new book, *Come Up Higher! Rediscovering Throne Life—The Highest Christian Life for the 21st Century*, is a powerful book which makes clear to the reader the importance of the subject, the fact that this is not a new subject but the theme goes back to the early church (Chrystostom), and has been promoted by some of the most important Christian writers in the Church's history.

Dr. King quotes from the Puritans: Thomas Watson, Thomas Brooks, William Gurnall ; Roman Catholics: Teresa of Avila, Thomas Aquinas; Baptists: Charles Spurgeon, F. B. Meyer; A.J. Gordon, E.W. Kenyon; Christian Missionary Alliance: A.B. Simpson, A.W. Tozer, John MacMillan, F.F. Bosworth; Pentecostals: Smith Wigglesworth; Presbyterian: A.T. Pierson, and many more famous people from many denominations.

If the book was a sermon, it would be a diamond sermon having one point but many facets. Dr. King looks at the subject of Throne Life from sixteen vantage points following the introduction. Though each chapter with its vantage point was helpful and interesting to me, I especially enjoyed Chapter 5—Throne Authority and Influence, Chapter 8—Throne Prayer, Chapter 13—Throne Faith, Chapter 14—Throne Holiness, and Chapter16—Throne Health and Healing.

Dr. King's corrections to abuses involving prosperity, and a recent emphasis on ruling with Christ due to our imputed righteousness without need for imparted holiness, is addressed powerfully, drawing upon the statements of these great leaders in Throne Life or the Higher Life of holiness. Paul King reminds us of the necessity of holiness to truly enjoy the authority of being seated with Christ in heavenly places.

This book is needed today, bringing a needed insight to the Church today of its privilege of ruling and reigning with Christ. And, at the same time, it reminds some of the younger leaders today of the wisdom of those who actually rediscovered these concepts (finished work - throne life - higher life - imputed righteousness), that there is also a need to have imparted what has been imputed, and to walk out our authority with humility and hearts of servants. Paul King reminds us of the need for holiness of heart to go with power and authority of positional righteousness.

This is not just a recommendation of the book; it is a recommendation of the man. I recommend Dr. King as a scholar, a man of integrity, a man of wisdom, a man whose heart is set on Jesus. He is a minister of The Christian Missionary Alliance, but like Wesley, he sees the whole world as his parish. I have enjoyed reading this book as well as his book, *Only Believe*.

—Randy Clark
Founder and President of Global Awakening
and the Apostolic Network of
Global Awakening
Author of *There Is More!*

Higher Ground

By Jonathan Oatman, Jr.

I'm pressing on the upward way
New heights I'm gaining every day
Still praying as I onward bound
"Lord, plant my feet on higher ground."

Chorus:

Lord, lift me up and let me stand
By faith on heaven's table land
A higher plane than I have found
Lord, plant my feet on higher ground.

My heart has no desire to stay
Where doubts arise and fears dismay
Tho' some may dwell where these abound
My prayer, my aim is higher ground.

COME UP HIGHER

I want to live above the world
Tho' Satan's darts at me are hurled
For faith has caught the joyful sound
The song of saints on higher ground.

I want to scale the utmost height
And catch a gleam of glory bright
But still I'll pray till heaven I've found
"Lord, lead me on to higher ground."

The Rich Heritage of Throne Life

"I press on toward the goal for the prize of the upward call of God in Christ Jesus" (Phil 3:14).

This verse from Philippians has been my life Scripture, the passion of my life. This is what the Higher Christian Life is all about. Jonathan Oatman's classic 19th century song "Higher Ground" was the theme song of the Higher Life Movement, expressing this desire yearning for the heavenly life, the throne life.

I dream of the day when the entire church of Jesus Christ would catch the vision of the highest Christian life. It would transform and unite the church. When everyone dies to self and exalts Jesus, denominational divisions and theological debates fade away as everyone looks to the throne and lives Throne Life. It is a message the whole church needs. For this purpose I have written this book. This is my heart, to bring to maturity and fullness in Christ every believer and every church.

In *Come Up Higher!*, I have sought to combine the best of classic teaching from many church backgrounds on the higher Christian life along with fresh insights and application for twenty-first century believers. Throne Life is the rich heritage of the Christian life throughout church history.

Concepts of Throne Life are not recent novel inventions. The theme of Throne Life was an ancient biblical truth based on Ephesians 2:6, identification with Christ by being seated with Christ in the heavenly places. These concepts were taught in various ways and terminology throughout church history, but became a lost treasure. Glimpses of the concepts of Throne Life can be found in early church fathers such as **Ignatius of Antioch** and **Chrysostom**, as well as medieval mystics such as **Hildegard of Bingen, Bernard of Clairvaux,** and **Teresa of Avila**.

The concepts were rediscovered and taught in some ways among the Puritans in the 17th and 18th centuries like **Thomas Traherne, Thomas Brooks, Thomas Watson**, and others. The teachings were especially recovered and popularized in the late 19th and early 20th centuries, permeating the Scotch and Dutch Reformed Covenant Theology, Keswick, Higher Life, and Overcomer movements.

The Higher Life movement appears to have begun with a book written in 1858 by Presbyterian minister **William Boardman**, entitled *The Higher Christian Life.* That book impacted Quaker evangelists **Pearsall and Hannah Whitall Smith**, the latter who wrote the classic *The Christian's Secret of a Happy Life* in the 1870s. Boardman, the Smiths, and others gathered together for a faith and holiness convention in the town of Keswick, England, in 1874. Thus the Keswick holiness movement emerged from that meeting, focusing on sanctification, the deeper and higher life, faith, and later on healing.

A.B. Simpson, another former Presbyterian minister, was profoundly impacted by Boardman's book. Simpson founded The Christian and Missionary Alliance (C&MA) in 1887, as a Higher Life movement emphasizing a Fourfold Gospel of Jesus Christ as Savior, Sanctifier, Healer and Coming King. A.B. Simpson wrote *The Highest Christian Life*, an exposition on Ephesians, as well as other books with related themes such as *In Heavenly Places, A Larger Christian Life*, and *Land of Promise.*

George Peck, a Methodist friend of Simpson and Baptist pastor A.J. Gordon, and a leader in the early C&MA, wrote his book *Throne-Life, or The Highest Christian Life*, in which he wrote concerning "throne-power," or the "command of faith."[1] This appears to be the premier book on the concept of Throne Life. After that came a proliferation of articles and sermons from various writers and preachers, popularizing the concept of Throne Life. **George D. Watson**, a Methodist holiness conference speaker, in the late 1800s wrote *Bridehood Saints*, which included a chapter entitled "The Hand on the Throne" (see chapter 8 on Throne Prayer).

Andrew Murray, a Dutch Reformed missionary to South Africa, wrote about this higher Christian life, what he called "the power of an endless life," in *The Holiest of All*, his great devotional exposition of the book of Hebrews. Based on Reformed Covenant theology, Murray and Simpson, as well as Swiss healing leader **Dorothea Trudel**, and the famed Scottish preacher and hymn writer **Horatius Bonar**, taught that believers are kings and priests.

Several Baptists leaders alluded to themes of Throne Life, or the higher Christian life, including **Charles Spurgeon**, British Keswick leader **F.B. Meyer**, American Baptists **A.J. Gordon** and **E.W. Kenyon**. **Oswald Chambers** taught principles of the higher Christian life in *My Utmost for His Highest* and other works, although he also warned of dangers and imbalances that can accompany the Higher Life movement.

Other leaders in the Keswick movement, cousins of the Higher Life movement, taught elements of Throne Life, such as Presbyterian preacher **A.T. Pierson**, who served as interim pastor of Spurgeon's Metropolitan Tabernacle, after Spurgeon's death. In 1906, Keswick and Overcomer movement leader **Jessie Penn-Lewis** (known as the "little apostle of England") wrote a booklet entitled *Throne Life of Victory*, which was hailed as "God's answer to powers of darkness." Keswick missionary to India **Amy Carmichael** alludes to the concepts of Throne Life, as well as **T. Austin Sparks, Norman Grubb**, and **Watchman Nee** in his books *Sit, Walk, Stand* and *God's Plan and the Overcomers*.

John A. MacMillan, a missionary and professor with The Christian and Missionary Alliance, wrote the classic book *The Authority of the Believer*, based on the principles of Throne Life. MacMillan's principles on the authority of the believer have been applied by a wide diversity of Christian leaders, including Kenneth Hagin, Billye Brim, and Kenneth Copeland in the Word of Faith movement, Wesleyan holiness leader Paul Billheimer, Foursquare leader Jack Hayford, and Freedom in Christ Ministries founder Dr. Neil T. Anderson.

Other C&MA leaders, such as **J. Furman Miller** and **Edith Beyerle**, popularly preached and wrote on themes of Throne Life. **A.W. Tozer**, while not using the terminology "Throne Life," nevertheless taught Throne Life principles out of his heritage in the Higher Life movement, especially through his classic book *The Pursuit of God*.

Sarah Foulkes Moore, co-founder and editor with her husband of an overcoming life magazine called *Herald of His Coming*, wrote a popular tract entitled "Throne Rights." Other 20th century Higher Life teachers teaching Throne Life principles include **F.J. Huegel**, missionary to Mexico, in *The Cross of Christ—The Throne of God* and *Bone of His Bone*; **DeVerne Fromke** in *The Ultimate Privilege, The Ultimate Intention*, and *Unto Full Stature*; and **Ruth Paxson**, in *Life on the Highest Plane*. More recently, Wesleyan holiness leader **Paul Billheimer**, taught themes of Throne Life in his popular books *Destined for the Throne* and *Destined to Overcome*.

Dr. Neil T. Anderson, founder of Freedom in Christ Ministries, makes use of Throne Life principles in his emphasis upon our identity and victory in Christ, in his ground-breaking books *The Bondage Breaker, Victory Over the Darkness*, and *Who We Are in Christ: A*

Devotional, and he acknowledges the influence of John MacMillan's classic book *The Authority of the Believer* upon his thinking.

Kris Vallotton and **Bill Johnson** have captured the vision of Throne Life for the 21st century in their powerful books *The Supernatural Ways of Royalty* and *Spirit Wars*. My friend and colleague **Joe McIntyre** has recently written a 21st century version of *Throne Life*, taking the basic concepts presented by George Peck and teaching them in a simple, understandable, but profound way for modern readers. I encourage you to purchase his book as a companion to *Come Up Higher*.

On a personal note, while researching and writing this book, I have often questioned whether or not I should be writing a book on Throne Life, because I live it so imperfectly. I don't always live on the throne. I have frequently thought that maybe a more spiritual, more holy person should write this book. Yet God keeps reminding me that it was He who placed writing this book upon my heart.

And so, obedient to the Lord to write in spite of my sense of unworthiness to do so, I press on toward the throne-ward call of God. I am in process, making progress to live consciously on the throne moment-by-moment, day-by-day. I am not there yet, but I am getting there more frequently, writing as a fellow pilgrim.

Join together with me in this journey into the Higher Life in Christ!

CHAPTER 1

Lifted to the Heavenlies

"God . . . seated us with Him in the heavenly places in Christ Jesus" (Eph 2:6).

"Heaven has received Him, and us in Him; we belong there."
—Andrew Murray[2]

In the book of Revelation, Jesus bids John, "Come up here" (Rev 4:1). Today Jesus is likewise calling us, "Come up higher. Join me at My throne." Every human being is called to a higher life—eternal life in Jesus. Every believer is called to a still higher life, life at the throne of God. If we can understand it, we are already there! Paul amazingly claims, "We have been seated in heavenly places."

Can you imagine that? As believers in Jesus Christ, we have been seated in the heavenly places! It is beyond our imagination!

In fact, it is so much beyond our understanding that when I ask an audience of people if they have heard of the phrase "Throne Life" or "Throne Power", usually no more than one or two hands go up. It is not a concept that is known or much taught in the 21st century.

When I was diagnosed with rectal cancer in 2007, I did not know if I was going to live or die. I sure did not feel like I was in heavenly places. Soon after hearing of the diagnosis of cancer, I received an encouraging phone call from Paul Hull, a retired pastor friend, which helped to change my perspective, attitude, and replies when people asked how I was doing. He told me of a card he had seen, which said on the outside, "Look down." I did not understand what my friend meant—"What do you mean, 'Look down.' Aren't you supposed to be encouraging me to look up? Then he explained that on the inside of the card were the words, "You are seated in heavenly places." He was encouraging me that I was seated above the worst of life with Christ in the heavens.

That is what this book is about—looking at life from the throne of God, where we are seated in the heavenly places. Sometimes when we are going through a trial, people ask us, "How are you doing?" And we reply, "OK, *under* the circumstances." However, we shouldn't be under our circumstances, or looking around at our circumstances, but looking down on them, for we are, indeed, seated in heavenly places—above our circumstances. It is a mountain-top perspective, not a view from the valleys of our life.

You Are Destined to Soar!

You may have heard the old story about the eagle who thought he was a turkey. A baby eaglet fell out of his lofty nest on to the ground among a bunch of baby turkeys. The momma turkey raised him with the other turkeys. As he grew, he would watch the eagles soaring, and he so desired to soar with them. The other turkeys told him, "You are wasting your time. You are a turkey, not an eagle. You will never soar." But he determined he was destined to fly, and one day threw himself off a cliff. And lo and behold! He did fly. He soared like an eagle, because he was one. He did not pay attention to what others had said. In his heart he knew his destiny was to soar. So it is with every believer in Jesus Christ. We are destined to soar and be seated in the heavenly places in Christ.

This is what the old holiness Higher Life writers called "Throne Life" or "Throne Power." This concept of "Throne Life" is one of the foundational principles of the classic faith understanding of the authority of the believer.

Beam Me Up, Scotty!

The Apostle Paul assures us, "For He rescued us from the domain of darkness, and transferred us to the kingdom of His beloved Son" (Col 1:13). The Greek word for "transferred," means "to carry across" or "to transfer location." In Star Trek language, we have been "beamed up" from the darkness of earth to the kingdom of heaven!

The early church father Chrysostom was astounded by this truth, commenting on Ephesians 2:6, "Amazing how He has raised up the Church! As if He were lifting us by a machine, He has raised us up to a vast height and installed us on that throne. . . . If a diadem, a crown of gold, was placed on our head, would we not do every thing that would seem worthy? But now, what is far greater, Christ is made our very head. . . . Conceive for yourself the royal throne; conceive of the excess of the honor!"

Think of that: "Conceive for yourself the royal throne!" Throne Life—we are lifted to a life out of ourselves, beyond ourselves; not our life, but Christ's life in us and through us. It is not we who lift ourselves, but Jesus Himself lifts us up to be seated with Him on the Father's Throne.

We Are Lifted by the Death and Resurrection of Jesus. F.J. Huegel declares the ancient truth that the Cross of Christ is the Throne of God. Apostolic Father Ignatius of Antioch, writing about 107 A.D. to the church at Ephesus, built upon the Apostle Paul's teaching to the Ephesians on the higher life nearly fifty years earlier. He declared, "You are stones of a temple, prepared beforehand for the building of God the Father, hoisted up to the heights by the crane of Jesus Christ, which is the cross, using as a rope the Holy Spirit; your faith is what lifts you up, and love is the way that leads up to God." The term "hoisted up" translates the Greek term *anaphero*, which means "to carry up higher" to the heights. He is saying that the work of the Cross, the atonement, carries us to a higher plane of life. Our faith is what enables us to go higher. In *The Holiest of All*, Andrew Murray explains:

> We have Jesus as our Forerunner into God's presence, with all the power of His death and resurrection-life working in us, and drawing and lifting us with divine energy into the Father's presence. Yes, Jesus with His divine, His heavenly life, in the power of the throne in which He is seated, has entered into the deepest ground of our being, where Adam, where sin do their work, and there is increasingly carrying out His work of lifting us heavenward into God's presence, and of making God's heavenly presence here on earth our portion.

Jessie Penn-Lewis likewise rediscovered this ancient truth, teaching on the believer's position in Christ according to Ephesians 1 and 2: "The Cross is the gate into this heavenly sphere, so that if the Holy Spirit reveals to us that when we are submerged into the death of Christ, we are loosed from the claims of sin, the flesh, and the devil, He will as certainly impart to us the life of the Risen Lord. He will lift us in real experience into our place in Him, seated with Him in the heavens far above all principalities and powers . . . far above the powers of darkness."[3]

We Are Lifted by Faith Like the Law of Lift Overcoming the Law of Gravity. As cited above, Chrysostom asserted, "Your faith is what lifts you up." He uses the Greek term *anago*, meaning to lead up to a higher place. This is just as the Apostle John declared that faith "is the victory that has overcome the world" (1 John 5:4). Even before the age of the airplane, Higher Life leaders envisioned faith as the "law of lift" spiritually. Hannah Whitall Smith illustrated this vividly: "Birds overcome the lower law of gravitation by the higher law of flight; and the soul on wings overcomes the lower law of sin and misery and bondage by the highest law of spiritual flying. The 'law of the spirit of life in Christ Jesus' must necessarily be a higher and more dominant law than the law of sin and death; therefore the soul that has mounted into this upper region of the life in Christ cannot fail to conquer and triumph."[4]

We Are Lifted by Contact with God Like a Magnetic Force. Seventeenth-century Puritan leader Thomas Watson cites Ezekiel 3:14, "The Spirit lifted me up," explaining that we are lifted by the "magnetic power of God's Spirit. The Spirit has not only a soul-purifying power—but a soul-elevating power. As the sun draws up the vapors from the earth—so the Spirit draws up the heart to God. . . . A Christian in this life is both *checked* and *spurred*; grace spurs him forward in his way to heaven, and then corruption checks him. But the Spirit comes in and draws up the heart to God; which is a mighty power—as if you should see a mill-stone drawn up into the sun."[5] For Baptist Keswick leader F.B. Meyer, to come into contact with God is to encounter a magnetic force that pulls us up to a higher dimension of living, as he prayed, "Human souls who touch You become magnetized, charged with a spiritual force which the world can neither oppose nor resist."[6]

We Are Lifted by God's Grace. Higher Life writer Sarah Foulkes Moore, in her booklet *Throne Rights*, explains: "Through the grace of God, every believer is elevated with Him to the right hand of God and occupies potentially the Throne of the Lord. In the purposes of God this elevation took place at the resurrection of the Lord Jesus Christ through the believer's identification with Him.[7] Puritan Thomas Watson likens the lifting power of grace with three vivid images:

★ *Grace carries us like a heavenly chariot:* "A godly Christian begins his heaven here, grace translates him into the paradise of God. Elijah left his mantle behind—but he was taken up in a fiery chariot. So it is with a saint, the mantle of the flesh is left behind—but his soul is carried up in a fiery chariot of love."

★ *Grace carries us upward like fire:* "Grace carries the soul up towards God. Grace is like fire. It is the nature of fire to *ascend*."

★ *Grace mounts us up on wings like eagles:* "You who lie *groveling on the earth*—feeding like the serpent, on dust—or like eels wrapping yourselves in the mud and slime of the world, had you that new and holy principle of grace infused, your souls would sparkle upwards—you would "mount up to heaven as eagles," Isaiah 40:31. Had you *the sharp eye of faith* to see Christ, you would soon have *the swift wing of desire* to fly to him."

We Are Lifted by the Life of Jesus Within Us. Jesus Christ has become a priest "according to the power of an indestructible life," the author of Hebrews declares (7:16). Andrew Murray comments on this verse: "These precious words are the key to the higher life. . . . His priesthood acts as an inner life within us, lifting us up. . . . Our High Priest by His life-power enters our life, and renews it, and lifts it up; His heavenly life becomes our actual life, and the presence of God surrounds and shines on us as the sunlight shines on our bodies." F.J. Huegel describes this identification with Christ as "swept forward by the tide of divine life, . . . spontaneously from the inner surgings of a heavenly life."[8]

We Are Lifted by the Love of God. Chrysostom also declared, "Love is the way that leads up to God." Again he uses the Greek term *anaphero*, meaning "to carry up higher." Love carries us when we cannot carry ourselves, when we cannot pull ourselves out of the pits of our lives. As the old hymn says, "When nothing else could help, love lifted me." Puritan philosopher Thomas Traherne asserted that through the true love of God, "you are advanced to the Throne of God."[9] An old hymn declares:

He has raised our human nature
On the clouds to God's right hand;
There we sit in heavenly places,
There with Him in glory stand.
Jesus reigns, adored by angels;
Man with God is on the throne;
Mighty Lord, in Thine Ascension
We by faith behold our own.

Think of this—He has raised our human nature. We are still human, but He has raised us above mere human nature. Imagine this: Man with God on the throne! We are seated on the throne with God. It is only by faith we can conceive of this truth.

Called to a Higher Life

As the Apostle Paul recognized the truth of this revelation, he knew that he had to make the revelation a reality in his own life: "Not that I have already obtained it or have already become perfect, but I press on that I might lay hold of that for which also I was laid hold of by Christ Jesus. . . . forgetting what lies behind and reaching forward to what lies ahead, I press on toward the goal for the prize of the upward call of God in Christ Jesus" (Phil 3:12-14).

Paul is not content with his spiritual life; he presses on higher. He has known Christ, but he wants to know Him still more. He has known the power of Christ's resurrection, but he desires to know that power still more. He has known what it is to share in the sufferings of Christ, but he wants to fellowship with those sufferings still more. And Paul bids us to follow His example: "Follow me as I follow Christ." Paul bids us along with him to come up higher.

Even in the Old Testament, God is always calling us to a higher life. Consider these verses:

"May the name of the God of Jacob set you securely on high!" (Ps 20:1).

"He makes my feet like hinds feet, and sets me upon my high places" (Ps 18:33).

"Who shall abide in Your tent? Who shall dwell on Your holy hill? He who walks with integrity and works righteousness, and speaks the truth in his heart" (Ps 15:1-2).

"But You, O Lord, be gracious to me and raise me up. . . . You set me in Your presence forever" (Ps 41:10, 12b).

Over and over again, we see that God's intention for His people is to live life on the heights; not in the valleys and lowlands, but on the hills of His holiness and presence.

Open the Eyes of Our Heart, Lord

Paul prays that the eyes of our heart may be enlightened (Eph 1:14-19). Understanding Throne Life can only come through divine enlightenment, not through human comprehension. Consider this: Paul is writing about this amazing truth while he is in prison. He is not in a very heavenly-like place. He is chained; he is restricted. Yet his spirit was not restricted. Even in chains, he is transported in his mind and heart to a heavenly realm in which he can see a deeper, fuller revelation of truth.

T. Austin Sparks explains that, like Paul, we need "a Divine apprehension and not merely a human appraisal of Paul's position." This is because "human levels of mentality would have produced an atmosphere of doubt, suspicion, question, and would have let in elements of false imputation. . . ." Therefore, it was especially while Paul was in prison that God revealed to him this "fullness of testimony from identification with Christ in death and resurrection, on to throne-union with Him, power over 'Principalities, Powers' etc., and on to the ministry 'in the ages to come.'"[10] We too today need a fresh revelation from God of our identity in Christ and our life with Him at the throne of God.

Why Stay in a Pit When You Can Sit on a Throne?

Even if you have chains in your life, even if you are seemingly restricted, held down or held back, those restrictions do not have to bind you spiritually. You are seated in the heavenly places. The 17th century French archbishop Francois Fenelon, whose writings influenced Higher Life thinking, counseled, "Don't live on the porch and think you are in the house."[11] God has much more for you. Through this biblical truth, God wants to see you throw off the shackles that hold you down. God wants you to soar like an eagle.

Charles Spurgeon understood this truth and challenges us today: "What fully enchants you to remain in a pit when you can sit on a throne? Do not live in the lowlands of bondage now that mountain liberty is conferred upon you. Do not be satisfied any longer with your tiny attainments, but press forward to things more sublime and heavenly. Aspire to a higher, a nobler, a fuller life. Upward to heaven! Nearer to God!"[12]

Therefore, as you read each chapter of this book, aspire to that higher, noble, fuller life to which Spurgeon challenges us. No matter where you are in your walk with God, no matter how long you have been a believer, no matter how high you have gone spiritually, God has something more for you—something higher, deeper, fuller:

- A dimension of the Spirit beyond the indwelling of the Spirit at your conversion.
- A dimension of the Spirit beyond the sealing, baptism, or filling of the Spirit.
- Something more God wants you to see.
- Something more God wants you to know.
- Something more God wants you to experience.
- Something more of God Himself.

I recommend that every day, you begin by personalizing the prayer of the Apostle Paul:

"Father of Glory, I pray that you will impart to me
the Spirit of wisdom and revelation
to open the eyes of my heart—
that I may more fully, deeply, intimately, know Christ,

that I may more fully, deeply, intimately,
know the hope of Your calling,
that I may more fully, deeply, intimately, know the riches of
Your inheritance for me,
that I may more fully, deeply, intimately,
know the exceeding greatness
of Your power and energy in my life."

CHAPTER 2

Entering The Throne-room— the Holy of Holies

"Esther put on her royal robes and stood in the inner court of the king's palace. . . . When the king saw Esther the queen standing in the court, she obtained favor in his sight; and the king extended to Esther the golden scepter. . ." (Esther 5:1-2).

The throne room is the innermost dwelling of the king, where only those who are his favored can approach. Throughout the Bible, God is pictured as a King, seated on a throne. "The Lord is in His holy temple; the Lord's throne is in heaven" (Ps 11:4). The picture is one of distance from the King. God's position on the throne is lofty and exalted, far above and beyond human capacity and comprehension. How can we dare approach the throne room of one so revered and exalted?

Yet God in all His glory bids us to approach Him, to enter the throne room, and to remain in His presence. He smiles upon us and lovingly calls us, "Come on in!"

Access to the Throne Zone—The Presence of the King

Esther gives us a picture of our approachability to the throne room of the King. She was not permitted to come to the king's chambers unless he had called for her. She dared to do so—only on the basis of the need and her relationship with the king. He extended the scepter to her and accepted her into his presence.

Through our identification with Jesus, we have the right of access to the throne room of the King of Kings. God our King has given us permission to access His throne room—His holy presence—through the blood of Jesus Christ. He has extended His scepter to us. Not only are we permitted in the throne room; we have the privilege of a personal audience with the King.

Amy Carmichael illustrates this truth in the way that she received leadings from God— through the special enlivening of Scripture in what she called a "durbar," an Indian word for a special personal audience with a high official, which she related to the Hebrew word *"dabar,"* to speak a word:

> When reading your Bible, have you not often noticed that some word has shone out in a new, direct, clear way to you? It has been as though you have never read it before. You cannot explain the vivid freshness, the life, in it, the extraordinary way it has leapt to your eye—to your heart. It just was so. That was the 'durbar'; you were in the very presence of your King at that moment. He was speaking to you. His word was spirit and life.[13]

This is what is sometimes called today a *"rhema,"* a special personal word from God. We have access to a personal word from the Throne of Heaven.

Access to Be Seated on the Throne

Not only do we have access to an audience with the King; as the Body of Christ we are given access to sit on the Father's throne with

His Son. This means that as Christ rules, we rule as co-regents. We are now with Christ on the throne as His body. When He returns in glory, we will be exalted even higher as we sit beside Him as His bride.

Access to the Throne of God Within— The Redeemed Human Spirit

Frances Ridley Havergal, the 19th century Higher Life hymn writer, in her hymn of consecration "Take My Life," recognizes that our heart is the very throne of God: "Take my heart, it is Thine own; it shall be Thy royal throne." Hannah Whitall Smith explains that like Elijah being translated into heaven through God's chariot of fire, the Higher Christian Life translates us "not into the heavens above, as Elijah did, but into the heaven within us. . . . These 'heavenly places' are interior, not exterior."[14]

These heavenly places are in our innermost being, our human spirit. When we are born again, the Spirit of God comes to dwell within our human spirit (Ezekiel 36:26). We become partakers of His divine nature (2 Pet 1:4).

Hildegard of Bingen, a 12th century abbess, writes that the Heavenly Jerusalem in the Book of Revelation "is a true symbol of what already exists in spirit today." Spanish medieval Christian mystic Teresa of Avila, like Havergal and Hildegard, viewed the human spirit as the throne of God, saying, "in the centre of the soul there is a mansion reserved for God Himself."

Theologian Herbert Lockyer likens the Holy of Holies to the human spirit of the believer: "The whole life of the believer is a trinity: The Outer Court, *the body*, connecting him with the world in which he lives; The Holy Place, *the soul*, where all its powers are priests serving Him; The Holiest of All, *the spirit*, where the Holy Spirit has His abode."[15] God has placed His throne in the innermost being of everyone who believes in Him.

Access to the Throne—Through the Cross

Our access to throne of God, the Holy of Holies, is through the Cross of Jesus Christ. A.B. Simpson assures us, "If you are to sit with Christ upon His throne, you must go through His Gethsemane."[16] Jessie Penn-Lewis taught on the believer's position in Christ according to Ephesians 1 and 2: "The Cross is the gate into this heavenly sphere, so that if the Holy Spirit reveals to us that when we are submerged into the death of Christ, we are loosed from the claims of sin, the flesh, and the devil, He will as certainly impart to us the life of the Risen Lord. He will lift us in real experience into our place in Him, seated with Him in the heavens far above all principalities and powers . . . far above the powers of darkness."[17]

Access to the Throne—Through a Contrite, Humble Heart

According to Scripture, we have access to the throne of God, not by exalting ourselves, but by humbling ourselves: "For thus says the High and Lofty One Who inhabits eternity, whose name is Holy: I dwell in the high and holy place, with him who has a contrite and humble spirit." (Isa 57:15, NKJV). Puritan Thomas Brooks comments, "The highest heavens and the lowest hearts are the habitations wherein the Holy One delights to dwell." The way up is down. Jessie Penn-Lewis explains:

> The triumphant Lord on the Throne now calls His church to enter into His death, and His life, and His Throne Life of victory. Let the believer who has been translated out of the power of darkness into the Kingdom of the Son now yield to the Holy Ghost to be drawn into the death of Christ, until in deepening conformity to His death he becomes assimilated to Him in vital union, even to oneness with His melted and broken heart.[18]

Access to the Throne—Through Delighting in the Lord

Delighting in the Lord leads to higher spiritual ground. Isaiah prophesied, "Then you will take delight in the Lord, and I will make you ride on the heights of the earth" (Isa 58:14). Alluding to Jacob's dream of a ladder to heaven, Thomas Traherne muses, "Our Savior's Cross is a Throne of Delights. . . . The Cross of Christ is the Jacob's ladder by which we ascend into the Highest Heavens." Jesus has opened heaven to us. Praising the Lord causes us to rise above our distress and ascend into heavenlies, to the Throne of Delights!

Entering into the Heavenly Throne Room— The Holy of Holies

"I saw the Lord sitting on a throne. . . my eyes have seen the King, the Lord of hosts" (Isa 6:1, 5)

"We have confidence to enter the holy place by the blood of Jesus" (Heb 10:19)

Isaiah entered the heavenly throne room, the Holy of Holies, through a special theophany, a supernatural appearance of God. However, through the blood of Jesus Christ, we have access to the heavenly throne room at any time.

While we have access to the throne room, we do not rush right into the throne room. We enter through the Outer Court, then progress into the Inner Court, the Holy of Holies, then into the Holiest of all. Earlier in our Christian lives, we tend to linger in one of these rooms before moving into the next. Or we step into the next room for a short period of time, then step back again. As we progress in our spiritual maturity, we move through these rooms more easily and swiftly, and dwell deep in God's presence.

Through the Outer Court—Where Jesus Is Given a Preferred Place. First, we enter the gates into the Outer Court, the place of thanksgiving, praise, testimony: "Enter His gates with thanksgiving, and His courts with praise" (Ps 100:4). The Outer Court is the general temple grounds, the place of repentance, where the blood is shed on the altar of sacrifice. Herbert Lockyer describes the Christian's life in the Outer Court:

> Associated with a deep desire in the heart of a born-again person for a richer experience of God's most perfect salvation is a growing spiritual apprehension of the glorious inheritance he has in Christ. . . . Those who give Him a preferred place— they are 'Outer Court Christians.' They entered through the gate and came to the brazen altar, signifying their salvation by the blood, and to the Laver, typifying their experience of the Spirit's regenerating work.[19]

The Outer Court is a wonderful place. It corresponds to the body of a human being created in the image of God. The Outer Court is a place of action, celebration, joy, and excitement for the redemption Christ has provided for us. In the Outer Court we engage in a lot of body motion—we may dance, clap, jump, or shout. The Psalms encourage us to do all of this.

The danger is in becoming satisfied with the Outer Court and not seeking to move on in. Lockyer laments, ". . . but, alas! They remain all their days in the Outer Court, as if deliverance from past guilt and regeneration were all God has for them."[20] Likewise, Andrew Murray prods us on: "There are outer-court Christians, who trust in Christ who died on Calvary, but know very little of the heavenly life, or near access to God, or service to others." He declares it "a call to all luke-warm, half-hearted Christians, no longer to remain in the outer court of the tabernacle, content with the hope their sins are pardoned."

Through the Inner Court—The Holy Place. God wants to take us further—into the Inner Court, the Holy Place. The Inner Court was the tent, the shelter containing the Holy Place and Most Holy Place. The Greek term for the Holy Place was *naos*, the temple. The physical body of a believer was called a *naos*, the temple of the Holy Spirit (1 Cor 6:19). The church (that is, the people of God, not a building) is a *naos*, the temple of the Holy Spirit (1 Cor 3:16; 2 Cor 6:16; Eph 2:21-22), just like the individual believer.

The Holy Place is a place of consecration and surrender, purity and cleansing. The Holy Place corresponds to the soul, comprised of our emotions, mind, and will. In the Holy Place our physical actions are more subdued—we kneel in the presence of holiness and the Holy One and our hands are raised in surrender.

The three objects in the Holy Place represent these three aspects of the soul. In partaking of the showbread, literally, "the bread of presence," our emotions are involved, sensing the presence of God. The lighting of the seven-branched candlestick or menorah represents the inner light, that is, the illuminating of our mind by the Holy Spirit. The offering on the Altar of Incense symbolizes offering ourselves in surrender to God as an act of our will.

The Holy Place, Lockyer describes, is where Jesus is given a "Prominent Place":

> They are 'Holy Place Priests,' who manifest delight in Him. They look upon the altar and the laver as the starting places of their journey heavenwards, but not as the end. They pass to and fro like the priest of old, serving the Lord in various ways. Knowing that there is more to follow, they enter the veil and learn the secret of His illuminating power as the candlestick, of His sustaining, strengthening life as the showbread, and of His mighty, prevailing intercession as the golden altar of incense.[21]

We might think that dwelling in the Holy Place is more than enough of God. After all, we experience His presence greater than ever before. We enjoy the illumination of the Spirit. We discover the power of prayer and intercession.

Yet, Andrew Murray stirs us still farther to recognize that God beckons us "not even to be satisfied with having entered the Holy Place and there doing the service of the tabernacle, while the veil still hinders the full fellowship with the living God and His love."

Into the Throne Room—The Holy of Holies. Murray explains that the "Holiest of All is the heavenly place." He called it "the heavenly sanctuary." The Holy of Holies is the innermost sanctum of our being—our spirit, the dwelling place of the Most High God. We have access to the Holiest. It is the place of ultimate worship, adoration, reverence, and awe. It is an abiding place—the place where we are to remain, to settle. This, Lockyer describes, is where Jesus is given the "Preeminent Place":

> They are 'dwellers in the Holiest of All.' Ever fewer in number, these aspiring saints ever strive to be filled with all the showbread of God. Life they have, but they desire its abundance. As the Most Holy place was the inner shrine filled with the presence of God, so all of them that hunger and thirst after Him reflect all unconsciously, as Moses did, the glory of His presence within their hearts. May you and I be found in this company! [22]

In the Holy of Holies, we have a full, implicit trust in God with not an iota of doubt. Our body and soul become totally at peace in stillness. Our body is so in awe, we fall on our face, humbled before the Almighty. It is a place of stillness: "Be still and know that I am God" (Ps 46:10, KJV). We find here, not the shouting of praises in the Outer Court, but a quiet ecstasy and peaceful contemplation. We experience a sweet intimacy with God that is indescribably delicious: "O taste and see that the Lord is good" (Ps 34:8).

The Holy of Holies is the place of the highest elevation in the spirit—the place of rarified air, in which we are left breathless in the presence of the Holy One. It is a place where we can see far from a mountain-top perspective. Our vision is unimpeded. We can there see the majestic vistas of the heavenly life in Christ. Lockyer describes this journey ever deeper into God's presence: "Then by the Holy Spirit we are led on within the veil until the beauties and glories of our adored and adorable Lord break bread upon our ravished souls."[23]

Imagine that!—The beauties and glories of our adored and adorable Lord! We think we have experienced beauty, but there is so much more! Andrew Murray envisions life in the Holiest:

> Oh the blessedness of a life in the Holiest! Here the Father's face is seen and His love tasted. Here His holiness is revealed and the soul made partaker of it. Here the sacrifice of love and worship and adoration, the incense of prayer and supplication, is offered in power. Here the outpouring of the Spirit is known as an ever-streaming, overflowing river from under the throne of God and the Lamb.

> Here the soul, in God's presence, grows into more complete oneness with Christ and more entire conformity to His likeness. Here, in union with Christ, in His unceasing intercession, we are emboldened to take our place as intercessors who can have power with God and prevail. Here the soul mounts up as on eagle's wings, the strength is renewed, and the blessing and the power and the love are imparted with which God's priests can go out to bless a dying world.

> Here each day we may experience the fresh anointing, in virtue of which we can go out to be the bearers, and witnesses, and channels of God's salvation to men, the living instruments through whom our blessed King works out His full and final triumph. O Jesus! Our great High Priest, let this be our life!

The Psalms of Ascent—Steps into the Throne Room. In the Book of Psalms, Psalms 120 through 134 are known as the "Songs of Degrees" or "Songs of Ascents" or "Songs of Going Up," using what is called in Hebrew poetry "stair-like parallelism." They were designed in a particular order in Jewish liturgy to describe worship as approaching the Temple through a series of spiritual steps. We go up by steps into the Holiest of Holies, ascending the mountain of the Lord, building toward climax.

Micah prophesied, "Now it shall come to pass in the latter days that the mountain of the Lord's house shall be established on the top of the mountains, and shall be exalted above the hills; and peoples shall flow unto it" (Micah 4:1, NKJV). In these latter days, people are rediscovering this Higher Christian Life and people are flowing into the heights and depths of the mountain of the Lord, the Holy of Holies. See how these psalms take us step-by-step into the Holy of Holies up the mountain of the Lord:

> 134—Continual worship in house of the Lord
> 133—Oneness with God—unity, anointing, bestowal of life
> 132—Ark comes into sanctuary—dwelling place
> 131—Quiet, composed trust in the Lord
> 130—Steady climb toward assurance
> 129—Reflections on where we have come from
> 128—Peace and blessing
> 127—On to the House of the Lord
> 126—Like a dream come true—from sorrow to joy
> 125—Security in Mount Zion
> 124—Sense of freedom
> 123—Look up to Mount Zion above the hills to God's throne in the Heavens
> 122—Joy of arriving at Jerusalem
> 121—Lifting our eyes to the mountains for help from the Lord
> 120—Begins in a distant land in distress and sin

Our spiritual journey into the Throne Room, the Holy of Holies, begins in a distant land, far from the heights and depths of the Christian life, crying to God in our distress and praying for God to deliver us and cleanse us from sin (Ps 120).

We see hope as we lift our eyes to the mountains for help from the Lord. As we journey on through our Christian life, when we keep our eyes on the goal of the upward call we are kept safe from the scorching heat of the sun and the troubles of darkness while journeying over the mountains (Ps 121).

As we draw closer, now standing within the gates of Jerusalem, the holy city, we proclaim, "I am glad when they said unto me, let us go into the house of the Lord," and we seek peace for our lives (Ps 122).

We go on to pray, "To You, I lift up my eyes, O You who are enthroned in the heavens!," and look to God for His graciousness in the midst of those who look upon us with contempt for our commitment to that deeper and higher life (Ps 123). When you seek more of God and less of the world, people will call you fanatics. They will scoff and try to dissuade you, trip you up, or sidetrack you in your journey.

We realize that "Had it not been the Lord who was on our side," we would have been overcome by the opposition against us, and we praise the Lord that He has secured our freedom from the snares of the enemy (Ps 124).

As we trust more fully in the Lord as our security and abide in Him, we are not shaken, but become as solid and immovable as Mount Zion. We grow in righteousness and experience the goodness of the Lord (Ps 125).

Although we experience setbacks and trials, as we experience greater release from spiritual and emotional bondage in the growth of sanctification, our hearts are filled with joy and our mouths with laughter—they who sow in tears will reap in joy (Ps 126).

We may revel in our joys, blessings, and prosperity, forgetting that "unless the Lord builds the house, they labor in vain who build it." We need to be reminded periodically in our spiritual journey that "it is vain for you to rise up early, to retire late, to eat the bread of painful labors." God wants us to reproduce ourselves spiritually, for "children are a gift from the Lord." (Ps 127).

Greater blessing comes as we grow in our reverence for the Lord. We will "eat of the fruit your hands, you will be happy and it will be well with you." Our blessing does not cause us to just sit and become complacent, but it bids us to continue walking in His ways further and higher and greater (Ps 128).

As we press on ever further and higher, we experience greater opposition. We pray for God to turn that opposition backward and to dry up the attacks (Ps 129).

In the midst of our trials, we pray, "Out of the depths I have cried to You, O Lord. Lord, hear my voice! Let Your ears be attentive to the voice of my supplications." We realize in a deeper way our own sinfulness and confess it to the Lord. As we wait upon Him and hope in His word, He grants us His loving kindness and redemption (Ps 130).

In this deeper work of sanctification, our pride and haughtiness is broken, and we confess, "O Lord, my heart is not proud, nor my eyes haughty; nor do I involve myself in great matters, or in things too difficult for me." We become like a weaned child and have composed and quieted our soul (Ps 131).

Our focus is no longer on ourselves, but we turn our attention upon seeking the dwelling place of God—the ark in the Holy of Holies. We gain a passion for the Holy Presence of God:

"Surely, I will not enter my house, nor lie on my bed; I will not give sleep to my eyes, or slumber to my eyelids until I find a place for the Lord, a dwelling place for the Mighty One of Jacob." We have a greater desire for worship at the very throne of God. We hear God speak to us in a fresh promise (Ps 132).

We are now on the mountain of God, the throne of the Holy One, in the Holy of Holies, the place where brothers dwell together in unity. The anointing of the Holy Spirit and the blessings of eternal life come upon us (Ps 133).

Psalm 134 gives us the climax of the ascent—the blessedness of continual worship of the Lord night and day in the Holy of Holies!

Hindrances to Entering in Holy of Holies

We are given free access into the Holy of Holies by the blood of Jesus, who has paved the way for us. What then hinders us from entering in and abiding in the Holy of Holies?

Not Knowing There Is More. First of all, we may not be aware that there is more. We have experienced joys in the Christian life and have thought this is it, we have arrived, there is nothing more. However, Paul bids us onward and upward. "I press on toward the goal for the prize of the upward call of God in Christ Jesus." (Phil 3:14).

Plateau and Complacency. If we become satisfied with where we are rather than pressing on for more of God, we become complacent. However, there is no plateau in the Christian life. If we are not going forward and upward, we are going backward and downward, even though we may not perceive it.

Acting in the Flesh. "Are you so foolish? Having begun by the Spirit, are you now being perfected by the flesh?" (Gal 3:3). We start out well in the Spirit, but we revert to the flesh. We have entered in before, but we cannot stay in because we have succumbed to our old nature.

Weights and Entanglements of Sin. "Let us also lay aside every encumbrance and the sin which so easily entangles us. . . ." (Heb 12:1). In the book and movie Lord of the Rings, the haunting attraction of the power of the Ring hindered Frodo.

Entanglements of Life. "Set your mind on the things above, not on the things that are on the earth" (Col 3:2). When our minds are set on earthly matters, we become chained to the earth and cannot soar as God intends. "No soldier in active service entangles himself in the affairs of everyday life, so that he may please the one who enlisted him as a soldier" (2 Tim 2:4). While we may be involved in the affairs of everyday life, we must not be entangled in them.

Anxiety and Fear. If we are afraid of the unknown, we will be immobilized, unable to move into the depths and heights of all God intends for us.

Feelings of Unworthiness. You may feel weak and unable and unworthy, yet Jesus bids you to enter into the Holy of Holies. Andrew Murray encourages us, "Even as Christ said to the man with the withered hand, 'Stand forth,' He calls to you from His throne in heaven, 'Rise and come and enter in with a true heart.'"

Let our prayer be the song of Dave Browning: "Take me past the outer court into the Holy Place. . . . Take me into the Holy of Holies."[24]

For Further Reflection

1. What keeps you from entering in and staying in the Holy of Holies?

2. What steps can you take to enter and abide in the Throne Room?

CHAPTER 3

View from the Throne— Understanding Our Throne Position

U nderstanding our throne position determines our attitude and disposition in life. If we do not realize or cannot conceive what it means to be seated on the throne of God in Christ, we cannot soar. We cannot experience the heights God has intended us to reach. We can only see life from the valley. However, once we view our lives from our position at the throne of God, we have a whole new perspective on life—a mountaintop view.

The Believer's Position in the Heavenlies

George Peck explains the two dimensions of our throne: 1) future— "On his future throne we shall be *personally* with Him; and 2) present—"on His present throne we are with Him *representatively*, in God's purpose and thought; *generically*, as we are born of Him; and *spiritually*, in conscious communion with Him, through His indwelling Spirit." Peck further distinguishes between three aspects of present throne position:

- ★ *Throne ways of being*—since we are born of God and we are united with Him—Christ is in us and we are in Him, and we are God's royal children.
- ★ *Throne ways of thinking*—as we sit with God on His throne representatively in God's purposes and thought, we begin to think throne thoughts—thinking as God thinks.
- ★ *Throne ways of living*—as we are in constant awareness of His presence and fellowship through the Spirit, we experience intimate communion with Him and the life of the throne.

Throne Ways of Being—Throne Union

"Throne union" is based on the union of the believer with Jesus Christ. As A. B. Simpson declares, "The Man who is in you now is a Heavenly Man." Tozer explains, "When God infuses eternal life into the spirit of a man, the man becomes a member of a new and higher order of being."[25]

Princes, Not Paupers. Simpson declares, "We have ceased to be paupers and have become princes."[26] A century later, Neil T. Anderson captures Simpson's thought: "Do you see the incredible kindness of our Lord in saying to a beggar who has known only rejection, 'Come, sit with me at my right hand'?"[27] Kris Vallotton and Bill Johnson have also expanded upon Simpson's vision in their book *The Supernatural Ways of Royalty*, writing chapters about "The Plight of Pauperhood" and "Castle Tramps or Palace Princes."

Because we are in Christ and Christ is in us, we are identified with Him in His death, resurrection, and ascension. Christ in us is the hope of glory (Col 1:27). We are united with Christ, bonded together with Him. By virtue of identification with Jesus Christ, we are seated with Him in heavenly places on the throne of God. A.B. Simpson describes Throne Life in this way:

This is much more than resurrection. It is ascension. It is taking the place of accomplished victory and conceded right, and sitting down in an attitude of completed repose, from henceforth expecting with Him until all our enemies be made our footstool. . . . It is throne life. It is dwelling with Christ on high, your head in the heaven even while your feet still walk the paths of the lower world of sense and time. This is our high privilege.[28]

As redeemed humanity, we are raised up to His level. Because we are His body, we are where He is; we ascend to where He ascends. We are dwelling on high with Christ. We are royal children of the King with full access to the throne. Throne Life is the Christ Life.

Throne Ways of Being—Throne Rest

Throne Rest Means Sitting, Not Striving. To be seated means a position of repose. It is a place of rest, not a place of striving. Watchman Nee notes we must be seated before we can walk or war: "The secret of a heavenly life—Christian life does not begin with walking; it begins with sitting. . . . We only advance in the Christian life as we learn first of all to sit down. . . . In the spiritual realm, to sit down is simply to rest our whole weight—our load, ourselves, our future, everything—upon the Lord. . . . Every time we reverse the divine order the result is disaster."[29]

He illustrates that being seated in Christ is like people who are sitting in an automobile. When the car is moving, the riders keep moving with the car even though they are in a state of repose. So when we are seated in Christ, when He goes we go; where He goes we go; what He does we do. J. Furman Miller, a Higher Life teacher with The Christian and Missionary Alliance, explains that all power flows from throne rest:

Successfully to wage our spiritual throne-warfare we must rest unreservedly in Christ's completed victory over all of Satan's forces on the Cross. Leave the fighting to Him, forsaking fleshly zeal for spiritual *rest*. Then labor ceaselessly to enter into that *throne-rest* from which all power flows. This is the only cure for sloth. The effort exercised is to the end that we be still and see the Lord perform, as we present our bodies to Him.[30]

How do we rest in warfare?—Through trust. When we are trusting God, we are in a state of resting. When I went through cancer, I learned to rest in the Lord all the while I was battling. That may seem like an oxymoron—to rest and battle at the same time.

Throne Rest Means Stillness. The Lord said to the Israelites, "Stand still while I gain the victory over the Egyptians." Sometimes we want to act, and God says, "Stand." We want to move forward— God says, "Stay where you are; hold your ground." Sometimes the victory is not in taking over new territory, but maintaining your hold on what you have now.

Yet while God told them to stand still, after He had taken action by rolling back the waters and blocking the Egyptians, He then told them to move—to walk through the Red Sea with walls of water piled high on either side of them. That takes considerable faith! This kind of faith only comes through being still before God, letting Him intervene in our behalf, then stepping out in trust.

Puritan Thomas Watson describes the joy and sweetness of throne rest, or "being still with God":

> To be still with God is the most comfortable life. What sweet harmony and music is in that soul? The bird, the higher it takes its flight, the sweeter it sings. Just so, the higher the soul is raised above the world—the sweeter joy it has. How is the heart inflamed in prayer? How is it ravished in holy meditation? What joy and peace in believing? (Rom 15:13), and these joys are those honey-streams which flow out of the rock, Christ! . . . He who is still with God—carries heaven about him. He has those tastes of God's love, which are the beginnings of heaven. So sweet is this kind of life, that it can drop sweetness into the troubles and afflictions of the world,

that we shall be scarcely sensible of them. It can turn the *prison* into a *paradise*; the *furnace* into a *festival*; it can sweeten death. A soul elevated by grace, can rejoice to think of dying: death will but cut the string, and the soul, that bird of paradise, shall fly away and be at rest.

Throne Rest Means Peace. Throne rest means that you can be at peace even when you don't have all the answers to your prayers; that you can take a Sabbath day off even when all your work is not done; that you can leave things be in the hands of others rather than micromanage. Teresa of Avila describes the peace and rest of those who dwell in the Holy of Holies, what she calls the "seventh mansion":

> A king resides in his palace; many wars and disasters take place in his kingdom but he remains on his throne. In the same way, though tumults and wild beasts rage with great uproar in the other mansions, yet nothing of this enters the seventh mansions, nor drives the soul from it. Although the mind regrets these troubles, they do not disturb it nor rob it of its peace, for the passions are too subdued to dare to enter here where they would only suffer still further defeat. Though the whole body is in pain, yet the head, if it be sound, does not suffer with it. [31]

Take hold of this truth now and declare: "I am seated on the throne of God as part of the body of Christ. Since Christ is seated, I am seated with Him. Since Christ is at rest and at peace, and I am in Him and He is in me, I declare that I am at rest; I am at peace in Christ."

Throne Ways of Thinking

Throne Worthiness—Think of Yourself as Worthy. We find it difficult to imagine that we are worthy to sit on the throne with Jesus at the right hand of God our Father. However, throne worthiness is not based on any spirituality on our part, but upon our union with Christ and our throne position with Him. Jesus Christ is the Worthy

One. We are worthy because He is in us and we are in Him. We are worthy because He is worthy.

John MacMillan, the pioneer in understanding and applying the authority of the believer, explains the concept of throne worthiness:

> The Emperor Napoleon, to emphasize the fact that it was possible in his service to rise from the lowest rank to the highest, made the epigrammatic remark that "every private soldier carried a field marshal's baton in his knapsack."
>
> And so the Almighty, as He sets forth the glories of the age to come and the surpassing magnificence of the eternal city, in which have been centered all the hopes of the ages as they ran their course, broadcasts to the race a similar announcement: "He who overcomes shall inherit all things"—a promise of joint-heirship with His overcoming Son; adding something still more lofty in its implications of blessing and divine fellowship: "I will be his God, and he shall be my son." As the inspired Psalmist, millennia before, stated the same truth: "He raises up the poor out of the dust, and lifts the needy out of the dunghill; that he may set him with princes, even with the princes of his people."
>
> There is no believer in Christ to whom the highest honors of heaven are not open. . . . The theology of the majority of pulpits teaches that all things are received in Christ, and fails utterly to insist on the need of "giving all diligence" in order to lay hold upon those graces and virtues which will never become the property of the saint without spiritual striving.[32]

Throne Ways of Thinking Give Us Throne Assurance. Puritan leader Thomas Brooks writes that assurance of salvation enables us to have a taste of heaven in the here-and-now:

> Assurance is the beauty and apex of a Christian's happiness in this life. It is usually attended with the strongest joy, with the sweetest comforts, and with the greatest peace. It is a pearl

that most want—a crown that few wear. His state is safe and happy, whose soul is adorned with grace, though he sees it not, though he knows it not. To have grace, and to be sure that we have grace, is heaven on this side of heaven.[33]

Throne Ways of Thinking Change Our Outlook on Life. F.J. Huegel writes of the new view from the heavenly heights: "From this rampart we look out upon life, conscious that we are set free from its petty strife. Race prejudices can no longer affect us. Class distinctions have been swept away. . . . Christ's cross has created for us a new and harmonious universe. Our love (the love of Christ constraining us) flows out in sympathetic yearnings for the welfare of all men."[34] He calls this new perspective "a look from the top." It changes who we are, what we think, and how we live.

Throne Ways of Living

Experience Throne Freedom. Jesus declared, "So if the Son makes you free, you will be free indeed" (John 8:36). We are in Christ; Christ is in us. In the heavenly places, Jesus Christ is free, unshackled, unbound. Therefore, because of our identification with Christ, we are unbound, unshackled—we are free indeed! Paul further explained, "Where the Spirit of the Lord is, there is liberty" (2 Cor 3:17). If we are in the Spirit, we are free.

Not Free to Sin, But Free Not to Sin. Throne freedom does not mean we are free to sin. Rather, it means we are free not to sin because we have died to sin through the death of Christ. "For he who has dead is freed from sin" (Rom 6:7). We are no longer slaves to sin. We don't have to sin. Paul declared that we do not have to let sin reign in our mortal bodies (Rom 6:12).

Throne freedom does not mean we can do what we want. Rather, it means we can do want God wants. Throne freedom does not mean we do not need to confess our sins. God's grace covers all our sins, but grace does not mean exemption from acknowledging our sins. To confess means to agree with, to acknowledge, to admit. When we confess our sins, we are agreeing that we have sinned and that they are covered by the blood of Jesus. Confessing our sins produces great freedom from guilt and condemnation.

Freedom to Be and Do All That God Intends. Throne freedom means that we are no longer chained, no longer bound to the lies that have built a prison around us. We are no longer limited by our past. We are no longer enslaved by addictions, no longer oppressed by condemnation. Throne freedom means that we are free to soar like an eagle as God intends. We are free to enter the Holiest of Holies, free to pursue unimpeded all the depths and heights of throne life in Christ.

Experience a Foretaste of Millennial Life. Thomas Brooks writes of the Puritan vision of the double blessing of experiencing heaven in this life as well as in the next life: "The being in a state of grace will yield a man a heaven hereafter; but the seeing of himself in this state will yield him both *a heaven here and a heaven hereafter.* It will render him doubly blessed—blessed in heaven, and blessed in his own conscience."

A.B. Simpson, sounding very much like the Puritans, spoke of Throne Life as a foretaste of what believers will experience in the Millennium after the return of Christ: "We are called to take the place which is to be ours after centuries have passed, and to look upon things as though we were already seated upon our millennial thrones and enjoying the glories and felicities of the ages to come."[35]

Experience the Powers of the Age to Come. Andrew Murray bids us experience the future age now:

> The more intelligently and believingly we abide in Him as our redemption, the more we experience, even here, of 'the powers of the world to come.' As our communion with Him becomes more intimate and intense, and we let the Holy Spirit reveal Him to us in His heavenly glory, the more we realize how the life in us is the life of the One who sits upon

the throne of heaven. We feel the power of an endless life working in us. We taste the eternal life. We have the foretaste of the eternal glory. . . .

Allow the powers of the coming world to possess us, and to lift us up into a life into the heavenly places, to enlarge our hearts and our views, to anticipate, even here, the things which have never enter the heart of man to conceive. [36]

Burn those words into your heart and mind, and open yourself to experience the powers of the age to come in the here-and-now!

Live Throne Life—Be an Incredible Christian!

A. W. Tozer understood throne ways of being, thinking and living, expressing the paradox of this Throne Life in his book *That Incredible Christian*:

The Christian believes that in Christ he has died, yet he is more alive than before and he fully expects to live forever. He walks on earth while seated in heaven and though born on earth he finds that after his conversion he is not at home here. Like the nighthawk, which in the air is the essence of grace and beauty but on the ground is awkward and ugly, so the Christian appears at his best in the heavenly places but does not fit well into the ways of the very society into which he was born.

The Christian soon learns that if he would be victorious as a son of heaven among men on earth he must not follow the common pattern of mankind, but rather the contrary. That he may be safe he puts himself in jeopardy; he loses his life to save it and is in danger of losing it if he attempts to preserve it. He goes down to get up. If he refuses to go down he is already down, but when he starts down he is on his way up.

He is strongest when he is weakest and weakest when he is strong. Though poor he has the power to make others rich, but when he becomes rich his ability to enrich others vanishes. He has most after he has given most away and has least when he possesses most.

He may be and often is highest when he feels lowest and most sinless when he is most conscious of sin. He is wisest when he knows that he knows not and knows least when he has acquired the greatest amount of knowledge. He sometimes does most by doing nothing and goes furthest when standing still.[37]

Tozer would challenge each of us to be that incredible Christian, to rise into the heavenlies above the world's ways of being, thinking, and living. Live Throne Life to the highest and fullest!

For Reflection

1. How can you personally experience throne rest?

2. How can you transform your mind to throne ways of thinking?

3. How can you live Throne Life as Tozer describes it?

CHAPTER 4

Our Throne Rights and Privileges

"But as many as received Him, to them He gave the right to become children of God, even to those who believe in His name" (John 1:12).

A pastor friend related to me that as a young pastor and evangelist, he experienced deep chronic depression. In fact, it was so debilitating in his life that his denominational superior did not want to recommend him for placement in a church or preaching as an evangelist. Then this pastor received a copy of a little booklet by Sarah Foulkes Moore, entitled *Our Throne Rights*, and it changed his life. As he began to realize his rights as a child of God, sitting as co-heirs on the throne of God, he began to claim and confess the believer's throne rights. As a result, within six months, the deep, dark depression had lifted never to return. The district superintendent then recommended him to churches and even came to him for counsel when his own son experienced deep depression.

We have great power to overcome the distresses of life when we understand the rights and privileges we have from the throne of God. When we give Christ His throne rights, dwelling in the high and holy place with a contrite heart, He grants us throne rights. Throne rights and privileges are based on throne position—in the heavenly places—the highest heavenly places far above all principalities and power.

Our Legal Rights to the Throne. As Paul Billheimer notes, "The Church, through her resurrection and ascension with Christ, is already legally on the throne."[38] Citing Paul's image of the church as the Body of Christ (Eph 1:19-23), Billheimer concludes, "If the Church as His body is organically united with Him as the Head, where does that place the Church? Can it be anywhere else except upon the throne with Christ? . . . We have already been legally enthroned with Christ because we are organically united with Him and have, therefore, already here and now entered upon our reign with Him. We are co-crucified, co-raised, co-exalted, co-seated with Christ. . . . All things are also legally beneath *our* feet."[39]

Our Rights as a Citizen of the Heavenly Kingdom. The Apostle Paul, as a Roman citizen, was born free. When he was on trial, he appealed to Caesar, which was his right as a citizen. He claimed "possession of his rights." Likewise, once we understand our rights as a citizen of the kingdom of heaven, we can claim possession of those rights.

Our Right to Wear the King's Robe. In the Old Testament book of Esther, King Ahasuerus honored Mordecai for foiling the assassination plot against him by giving Mordecai the right to wear the royal robes of the king (Est 6:7-11). He was treated as royalty. In a similar way, because of Christ's work of redemption in identification, as believers we take on the identity of the righteous Christ.

Paul declared, "He made Him who knew no sin to be sin on our behalf, so that we might become the righteousness of God in Him" (2 Cor 5:21). On this basis, Andrew Murray exhorted, "Believer, abide in Christ as your righteousness. . . . Take time to realize that the King's own robe has indeed been put on, and that in it you need not fear entering into His presence. It is the token that you are the man whom the King delights to honour. . . . Live your daily life in the full consciousness of being righteous in God's sight, an object of delight and pleasure in Christ."[40]

Speaking of God's grace to seat us in the heavenly places in Christ, A.W. Tozer writes, "We benefit eternally by God's being just what He is. Because He is what He is, He lifts up our heads out of the prison house, changes our prison garments for royal robes, and makes us to eat bread continually before Him all the days of our lives."[41] Think of that!—Prison garments to royal robes! In a similar vein, Simpson asserts:

> Do we dare to believe that we are absolutely, utterly, eternally accepted in Jesus Christ, in the same sense as He is accepted, and righteous even as He is righteous? Can we believe that our very name before God is: 'The Lord Our Righteousness;' His own name of ineffable holiness (Jer 23:6) given to us (Jer 33:16), even as the bride bears the husband's name? Now, this all comes by a simple act of believing God's testimony. God declares it of us simply because we have accepted Christ's atonement and we believe the declaration; and take the new place assigned us.[42]

This righteousness is known as *imputed* righteousness, reckoned to the believer and worn as a garment, not to be confused with *imparted* righteousness within the believer, which is related to sanctification. We have the right to wear the robe of righteousness, and as we grow in holiness, that righteousness is imparted within us.

Our Rights to Blessings in the Heavenly Places. According to the Apostle Paul, God "has blessed us with every spiritual blessing in the heavenly places in Christ" (Eph 1:3). This word "blessed" in Greek means that we have been blessed in the past once for all. It has already been done for us. Every blessing is available to us. However, it is only available in the *heavenly* places, not in the earthly. Someone once asked me, "Since we have already been blessed, don't we get it all? Potentially, yes. Ultimately, yes.

However, farther down in the chapter in verse 14, in the context we see the qualifier—the Holy Spirit is the *earnest*—the pledge or down payment of our inheritance. Every blessing is ours in the heavenly places, but what is available to us now is just the down payment. It is a huge, magnificent down payment beyond what we can imagine (Eph 3:21), but it is still just the down payment. There is much, much more to follow. We are mistaken if we think we get it all now.

On the other hand, most of us have not realized how gigantic a down payment we have received and have available to us now. Most of us are not cashing in on the full down payment. We don't understand the full extent of our rights, so we are living beneath our means in the heavenly life here-and-now.

Our Rights to Throne Inheritance. This is why Paul prays that we might *fully* know the riches of the glory of our inheritance. Paul uses a word for "to know" that means that we might *really, really* know— that we might perceive or discover. Not to know with our mind, but to know from experience, from intimate acquaintance with it.

It is a *glorious* inheritance. The Hebrew word for glorious means "heavy, weighty." It is no light-weight inheritance. It is not fluff. When we focus mainly on our inheritance as tangible prosperity, we are focusing on the fluff. Material riches are not the weighty part of our inheritance. "Glorious" also has the meaning of radiant, bright and shining. Our inheritance shines. It radiates the presence and power of God.

Exercising faith involves understanding who we are in Christ, our exalted position as a child of God. Simpson regarded knowledge of the believer's identity as a child of the King as vital: "How rich our inheritance as children of the King! How infinite our resources! How glorious our prospects! How we should dwell on high, above all low and groveling things, and bear the dignity of princes of heaven. . . . How unworthy to be living a life of discontent, strife and misery. 'All things are yours' (1 Cor. 3:21)."[43]

Our Rights to Throne Abundance. Jesus promised us, "I came that they may have life, and have it abundantly" (John 10:10). Abundant life, life to its fullest is the right of all who share the throne with the King. For every thing we need, Paul encourages us, "And my God will supply all your needs according to His riches in glory in Christ Jesus" (Phil 4:19).

Our Rights to Being the Head, Not the Tail. Based on Deuteronomy 28:13, people in covenant with God are "the head and not the tail, above and not beneath." Seventeenth-century Puritan leader Thomas Brooks claimed this Scripture, asserting that believers could in this life receive "outward riches, prosperity, and glory." Likewise, 19th century Baptist pastor Charles Spurgeon, known as "the last of the Puritans," also claimed this Scripture: "Though this be a promise of the law, yet it stands good to the people of God; for Jesus has removed the curse, but He has established the blessing. It is for saints to lead the way among men by holy influence; they are not to be the tail, to be dragged hither and thither by others. . . . Are we not in Christ made kings to reign upon the earth?"[44]

Our Rights to Our Authority as a Believer. MacMillan calls the authority of the believer the "heights of fellowship, of authority, and of victory." He declares that the believer can assert "in prayer the power of the Ascended Lord, and the believer's throne union with Him. . . . Where in faith the obedient saint claims his throne-rights in Christ, and boldly asserts his authority, the powers of the air will recognize and obey."[45] We will explore this further in the next chapter.

Our Right to the Throne Keys. Jesus promised the keys of the kingdom to His church: "I also say to you that you are Peter [*petros*— little rock], and upon this rock [*petra*—boulder] I will build My church; and the gates of Hades [Hell] will not overpower it. I will give you the keys of the kingdom of heaven, and whatever you shall bind on earth shall have been bound in heaven, and whatever you loose on earth shall have been loosed in heaven" (Matt 16:18-19).

The keys to the kingdom have been given, not just to Peter, but to the whole church. We have the authority to open and to shut, to lock and to unlock, to bind and to loose. We have authority to batter down the gates of hell with the battering ram of the Rock of our confession of Jesus Christ as the Messiah, the King of the Kingdom.

Our Right to Reign in Life. Paul writes, "Those who receive the abundance of grace and of the gift of righteousness will reign in life through the One, Jesus Christ" (Rom 5:17). On the basis of Paul's claim, Andrew Murray declares, "He has made us kings and priests. . . . Jesus fills us with a kingly nature. He enables us to rule over sin, over the world, over men."[46] Again Murray exhorted, "Let each disciple of Jesus seek to avail himself of the rights of the royal priesthood."[47]

Also commenting on this verse, Hannah Whitall Smith expands upon the theme: "What do we know of that *much more* reigning in life by Christ Jesus? . . . Do we reign over things much more than they once reigned over us? . . . We have been reigned over by thousands of things—by the fear of man, by our peculiar temperaments, by our outward circumstances, by our irritable tempers, even by bad weather. We have been slaves where we ought to have been kings. We have found our reign to be *much less* rather than *much more.* . . . We have been called to be kings, and we were created to have dominion over the earth (see Gen. 1:28)."[48]

Our Rights to a Hand on the Throne. George D. Watson, a 19th-century holiness leader, declared, "It is because the hands of the man Christ Jesus are on the throne that His prayer prevails, and through Him we lift up our hands and place them on the same throne, that we may prevail against all our enemies. . . . And when we, like Moses, lift up our hands and through Jesus lay them on the throne of grace, it is then we gain the day, . . . the Amalekites were conquered because the hands of a man were upon the throne."[49] We will explore this further in the next chapter.

More Promises of Throne Life

The Psalms are filled with rich images of the promises of God for experiencing Throne Life. Among them include the following:

* ★ ***The Promise of His Abiding Throne Presence.*** "He who dwells in the secret place of the Most High shall abide under the shadow of the Almighty" (Ps 91:1, NKJV). The secret place is the inner chamber, the throne room of the Most High. Psalm 41:12 tells us we are set in God's presence forever.

* ★ ***The Promise of His Throne Safety.*** "Because he has loved Me, therefore I will deliver him; I will set him securely on high, because he has known My name. He will call upon Me, and I will answer him; I will be with him in trouble; I will rescue him and honor him. With a long life I will satisfy him and let him see My salvation" (Ps 91:14-16).

  George Peck calls this "throne deliverance," help from the throne by which we are rescued and set on high. Oswald Chambers assures us, "The Lord Himself is our inviolable place of safety. There is a loftiness and an inaccessibility about the heavenly places in Christ Jesus. The higher you climb the purer the air until you come to the place where the least microbe is unable to live, and spiritually there is an inaccessible place of absolute security."[50]

* ★ ***The Promise of Throne Stability.*** "He makes my feet like hinds' feet, and sets me upon my high places" (Ps 18:33). The feet of the antelope are nimble and quick, so they are able to move safely from one rock to another without fear of stumbling and falling. God empowers us to move with agility and stability even when things seem uncertain in our lives.

* ★ ***The Promise of Living on the Throne Heights.*** "O Lord, who may abide in Your tent? Who may dwell on Your holy hill? He who walks with integrity, and works righteousness, and speaks truth in his heart" (Ps 15:1-2). When we have clean hands and

a pure heart, we dwell on God's holy hill. We experience the heights of God's presence and glory.

Hebrews 4:14 exhorts us, "Therefore, since we have a great high priest who has passed through the heavens, Jesus the Son of God, let us hold fast our confession." Then in verse 16, the author bids us, "Therefore, let us draw near with confidence to the throne of grace," and shows us three additional New Covenant promises of Throne Life:

- **The Promise of Approachability.** *Therefore, let us draw near with confidence. . ."* We can approach God with boldness, not fear or reserve. We have access to God (Eph 2:18). In the Old Testament, only the High Priest could enter into the Holy of Holies, and that only once a year. We have been given the right and authority to enter into the Holy of Holies daily (Heb 10:19-22).

- **The Promise of Mercy.** *". . . So that we may receive mercy."* Just as the king extended the scepter to Esther when she entered the throne room, so God extends His scepter of acceptance and mercy.

- **The Promise of Grace.** *"We . . . find grace to help in our time of need."* God's dwelling place is called the throne of grace. Grace is the unmerited power to overcome. God's grace is sufficient for every need (2 Cor 12:9). When he extended the scepter, the king asked Esther, "What is troubling you, Queen Esther? And what is your request? Even to half of the kingdom it shall be given to you" (Est 5:3). God extends His grace to whatever is troubling us. He desires to bless us, to give us His kingdom.

The Here Now and Not Yet of Our Inheritance

Our Inheritance Is Here Now. These vital words of Sarah Foulkes Moore emphasize the necessity of understanding that our throne authority which we inherit is not some future state, but here now:

For the Church of Christ to stand victoriously in this hour when satanic forces are united in full and deadly array against her, every believer must understand the necessity of NOW accepting with Christ the place of spiritual authority and fearlessly bind these forces of darkness, enforcing Calvary's triumph over them. In order to make the necessary advances in the work of the Kingdom at this hour, it is absolutely essential that believers, in humility, giving honor to God, take their seat in the heavenly places in Christ at His right hand, far above all powers of the air, and from that set hold them in subjection, through faith in the name and authority of Jesus.

We do not experience the kingdom now because we do not claim our kingdom now. We have left it for another day, another life. We often fall so short of what we can experience and claim in this life.

Limitations to Throne Inheritance—Not Fully Yet. Claiming our throne rights does not mean naming and claiming anything we want. It means naming and claiming anything *God* wants. We mistakenly think that because we have throne rights, we are entitled to a big house, a big car, fancy clothes and lots of toys and trinkets to play with. This is an adolescent view of claiming our throne rights.

Remember as a teenager, you wanted everything, and you wanted it ***now***. As a 12 year old, you may have said, "I want a car." But you were not ready for a car at 12. You may not have even been ready for a car at 16!

There is a time and a place for claiming our inheritance. We don't get our inheritance all at once, because we would not know how to handle it with maturity and wisdom. Thus, we can only claim what God shows us we are ready to handle.

Our throne rights ***do*** include claiming everything that we need. The problem comes when we confuse our needs with our wants. Not everything we think we need is what God thinks we need. Puritan William Gurnall counsels, "A wise father may bequeath a huge estate to his child—but not let him control any more of his inheritance than he can manage properly."[51]

Andrew Murray further explains that possessing our inheritance depends upon maturity:

> The death of the testator gives the heir immediate right to the inheritance. And yet the heir, if he be a minor, does not enter into the possession. A term of years ends the stage of minority on earth, and he is no longer under guardians. In the spiritual life the state of pupilage ends, not with the expiry of years, but the moment the minor proves his fitness for being made free from the law, by accepting the liberty there is in Christ Jesus.[52]

In similar fashion, A.J. Gordon aptly put it: "The promises of God are certain, but they do not all mature in ninety days."[53] So recognize what you can legitimately claim as your inheritance now, and what needs to mature in your life before you can receive a greater measure of that inheritance.

Claim Your Inheritance in Due Season. Spurgeon counseled that a believer can rightly claim a promise of inheritance only when it is "in due season":

> Often you cannot get at a difficulty so as to deal with it aright and find your way to a happy result. You pray, but have not the liberty in prayer which you desire. A definite promise is what you want. You try one and another of the inspired words, but they do not fit. You try again, and in due season a promise presents itself which seems to have been made for the occasion; it fits exactly as a well-made key fits the lock for which it was prepared. Having found the identical word of the living God you hasten to plead it at the throne of grace, saying, 'Oh Lord, Thou hast promised this good thing unto Thy servant; be pleased to grant it!' The matter is ended; sorrow is turned to joy; prayer is heard."

Once you know from the Lord that it is your due season—claim it, hold on to the promise, and give Him praise!

Life on Wings—Claim Your Rights to Soar in the Heavenlies!

Thomas Watson pictures the plight of many Christians, unable to soar in the heavenlies: "Like the ostrich, though she has wings, yet by reason of the weightiness of her body cannot fly high; most men are so weighed down with *thick clay* that they cannot soar aloft." However, we have a throne right to live above the life of sin and bondage and defeat. We have a throne right to live victoriously over temptation and trouble, even while we live in the midst of attack and harassment on our lives.

"Throne rights" means the privilege to live in the heavenlies in the here and now. We are not turkeys. We have a right to soar. It is in our nature. Like Puritan Thomas Watson, Hannah Whitall Smith describes it as "life on wings":

> The life hid with Christ . . . is life on wings—the wings of surrender and trust. . . . If we will only surrender ourselves utterly to the Lord, and will trust Him perfectly, we shall find our souls "mounting up with wings as eagles" to the "heavenly places" in Christ Jesus, where the earthly annoyances or sorrows have no power to disturb us. The wings of the soul carry it up into a spiritual plane of life, into the "life hid with Christ in God," which is a life utterly independent of circumstances, one that no cage can imprison and no shackles bind.[54]

Claim your inheritance today and pray: "I want to live above the world, where Satan's darts at me are hurled." Take flight and soar like an eagle in the heavenlies as God intends for you!

For Reflection

1. What throne rights do you have that you have not claimed?

2. What keeps you from soaring in the heavenlies?

CHAPTER 5

Throne Authority and Influence

"Behold, I have given you authority to tread on serpents and scorpions, and over all the power of the enemy. . ." (Luke 10:19).

The Overcoming Truth of Our Authority as a Believer

The promise of authority given to the seventy disciples is bestowed upon every believer. When we know the truth of our authority as a believer in Jesus, the truth sets us free (John 8:32). Recognizing and exercising my authority as a believer was crucial in my battle of overcoming cancer. If I had not acted in that authority, I would have succumbed to fear, doubt, worry, pain, and possibly to death itself. Understanding our authority as a believer is crucial in overcoming the trials and distresses of life, as well as gaining victory in spiritual warfare.

Creation Authority Levels. In order to understand our authority, we need to understand the creation hierarchy of authority set up by God. Authority is not intrinsic; it is delegated by God. We have no authority on our own. We only have authority as we are under authority so designated by God. God instituted a spiritual hierarchy at Creation:

God
↓

Angels and spirit world
(Ps 8:5; Eph 2:1-3)
↓

Humankind
(Gen 1:28)
↓

Creation[55]

God has authority over all. The angels and the spirit world were created higher in rank than humankind. As Hebrews 2:6-7 translates Psalm 8:5, "What is man, that You remember him? Or the son of man, that You are concerned about him? You have made him for a little while lower than the angels. . ." In turn, authority over the created earth was delegated to humankind at creation:

> Then God said, "Let us make man in Our image, according to Our likeness; and let them rule over the fish of the sea and over the birds of the sky and over the cattle and over all the earth, and over every creeping thing that creeps on the earth." God created man in His own image, in the image of God He created him; male and female He created them. God blessed them; and God said to them, "Be fruitful and multiply, and fill the earth, and subdue it; and rule. . ." (Gen 1:26-28).

You have crowned him with glory and honor, and have appointed him over the works of Your hands; You have put all things in subjection under his feet (Heb 2:7; Ps 8:5).

Men and women together were given dominion over creation. Early Church Father Clement recognized this authority in his prayer: "For you, Heavenly Master, King of the ages, give to human beings glory and honor and authority over the creatures upon the earth" (1 Clement 61:2).

Human Authority After the Fall. However, humankind lost much of that dominion with Adam and Eve's sin. Because of the Fall, humankind was deprived of much (though not all) of the dominion God intended. Fallen creation rebels against God's intention. That is why we are often afraid of wild animals and snakes. However, before the Fall, humankind had dominion over such creatures. Psalm 8 indicates that humankind still has that authority; however, it became difficult to exercise that authority. The rebellious evil powers claimed territory on earth and in the lives of humans.

Nevertheless, Daniel in the lions' den and Elijah stopping and starting rain are examples of recovering dominion over creation. Elisha exercised that same authority in sending the bears after the scorning youth and causing an axe head to float.

Recovering Dominion. By redemption through the cross of Jesus Christ, that dominion is once again fully restored to all humankind who believe in Him; that is, the Church. Andrew Murray asserted: "Church of the living God! Your calling is higher and holier than you know! God wants to rule the world through your members. He wants you to be His kings and priests. Your prayers can bestow and withhold the blessings of heaven."[56] Andrew Murray put into practice his own teaching, on one occasion taking authority over a pack of snarling wild dogs in the name of Jesus and walking through the midst of them unharmed.

What Gives You the Right? People may say, "What gives you the right? Who gives you authority? Who died and made you king?" As a matter of fact, Jesus, the Kings of Kings, died and rose and made us royalty. The Apostle John writes, "For as many as received Him, to them He gave the right [Greek, *exousia* = authority] to become children of God, even to those who believe on His name" (John 1:12). Since God is the King of kings and Lord of lords, we are a child of the King of Kings—we are princes and princesses. All believers have the rights and privileges of a child of the King. We are co-heirs with Christ (Rom 8:17).

Thus, the famed Scottish preacher and hymn writer Horatius Bonar can legitimately claim, "God is seeking kings. Not out of the ranks of angels. Fallen man must furnish Him with the rulers of His universe. Human hand must wield the scepter; human hands must wear the crown."[57]

Throne Hierarchy—Your Exalted Place in God's Hierarchy. At Jesus' resurrection, the spiritual hierarchy was changed. "For He rescued us from the dominion of darkness, and transferred us to the Kingdom of His beloved Son" (Col 1:13). Not only is humankind restored to dominion over creation, but believers in Jesus Christ, because we are His Body, are exalted above the spirit world. This is a different order of hierarchy than that of humankind at creation.

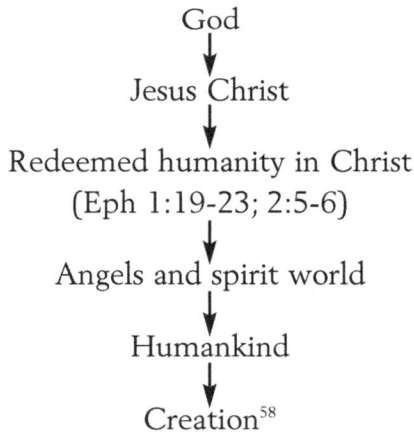

God
↓
Jesus Christ
↓
Redeemed humanity in Christ
(Eph 1:19-23; 2:5-6)
↓
Angels and spirit world
↓
Humankind
↓
Creation[58]

Jesus Christ, who had humbled Himself to the lowest rank (Phil 2:5-10), has been raised into the heavenlies and is seated at the right hand of God on His throne. All principalities, powers, dominions, and names have been put under His feet (under His authority) (Eph 1:19-23).

Further, when we are saved, we are seated with Christ in the heavenly places on the right hand of the throne of God (Eph 2:5-6). Oswald Chambers explains, "Remember, although Jesus Christ is on the throne, you are "prime minister" under Him."[59]

F. B. Meyer explained our place as believers in this new hierarchy of God: "Is Satan under Christ's feet? In God's purpose he is under ours also."[60] Since all things are under Christ's feet, and we are His body, therefore, all things are also under our feet!

Puritan writer William Gurnall likewise affirms this truth: "Let the saints humbly shout, 'Hallelujah!' When God made you a holy man or woman He gave you gates and bars to your city. . . . Once you were a timid slave to [Satan] but now he is under your feet. The day you became holy God firmly planted your foot on the serpent's head. . . . The devil can never lift his head—his wily schemes—higher than the saint's heels. He may make you limp, but he cannot take your life."[61]

The spirit world, both good and evil spirits, are therefore under our authority to the degree delegated by Christ. Ministering angels serve the saved (Heb 1:14). The evil spirit forces of wickedness are under our feet. Meyer illustrates this further:

> He gives us authority to tread on all the power of the enemy. As a man in uniform is able to regulate the traffic of a crowded street, because he represents the authority of the state, so the weakest child of God, who stands in the victory of Calvary, is able to resist and overcome all the power of the evil spirits, who infect the air.[62]

God's Law Enforcement Agency. Paul Billheimer elaborates on the legal authority of the believer, "God proposes—a holy church disposes. God's offer of His scepter to humanity is, therefore, a bona fide offer. . . . Through the plan of prayer God is actually inviting redeemed man into FULL partnership with Him, not in *making* the divine decisions, but in *implementing* those decisions in the affairs of humankind. . . . The responsibility and authority for the enforcement and administration of those decisions He has placed upon the shoulders of His Church. . . . God deputizes His Church."[63]

A.B. Simpson, an early teacher of the authority of the believer, used a policeman analogy of spiritual authority similar to F.B. Meyer:

"'I give you authority.' This is the policeman's badge which makes him mightier than a whole crowd of ruffians because, standing upon his rights, the whole power of the state is behind him. . . . Are we using the authority of the name of Jesus and the faith of God?"[64]

Paul Billheimer explains this as a dynamic synergy between God and the believer, in which God decrees in heaven, and the church executes God's decrees as His law enforcement agency on earth: "Heaven holds the key by which decisions governing earthly affairs are made, but we hold the key by which those decisions are implemented. . . . It is enforcing His will upon earth."[65]

Who?—Me? You may not feel worthy or spiritual enough to exercise this kind or extent of authority. John MacMillan assures us such authority is *not* "the property only of a few elect souls. On the contrary, it is the possession of every true child of God. It is one of the 'all things' received in Christ."[66] He further declares: "The weakest and the most unlettered saint is able, by the cross and its conquest of the powers of hell, to drive the fiercest 'bulls of Bashan' (Ps. 22:12) in headlong flight."[67] As F.B. Meyer encourages, "If only you can claim to be in the *feet* of the mystical body of the risen Lord, you can tread on serpents and scorpions and on all the power of the devil."[68] It does not matter how young or old a Christian you are, how mature you are, how long you pray or fast, you have this authority delegated from Christ.

How Much Authority Do I Have?[69]

We first need to clarify that God the Father has given Jesus *all* authority (Matt 28:18). No one else ever has all authority, only Jesus. It is vital to note that Jesus does *not* transfer or abdicate authority to believers, as some people have erroneously concluded. Rather, Jesus delegates authority to us. Any authority that we have is delegated authority and is constituted authority only in certain dimensions. However, those dimensions are often vaster than we have imagined. This throne power exercises the heavenly authority of the believer in the earthly circumstances of distress and disease. Some of the dimensions of authority we can exercise include the following:

Authority to Destroy Spiritual Strongholds. "For the weapons of our warfare are not of the flesh, but divinely powerful for the destruction of fortresses" (2 Cor 10:4).

Authority to Cast Out Demons and Heal. "Jesus summoned His twelve disciples and gave them authority over unclean spirits, to cast them out, and to heal every kind of disease and every kind of sickness" (Matt 10:1).

Authority to Advance the Kingdom of God. "And as you go, preach, saying, 'The kingdom of heaven is at hand'" (Matt 10:7).

Authority to Take Back Territory from the Enemy and Drive Satanic Forces Out of Our Household. "But if I cast out demons by the Spirit of God, then the kingdom of God has come upon you. Or how can anyone enter the strong man's house and carry off his property, unless he first binds the strong man? And then he will plunder his house" (Matt 12:28-29).

Authority to Bind Dark Forces of Evil and Loose Captives from Bondage. "Behold, I have given you authority to trample on serpents and scorpions, and over all the power of the enemy, and nothing will injure you" (Luke 10:19). Commenting on this verse, Jessie Penn-Lewis declared, "The soul hidden with Christ in God has authority over all the power of the enemy, for he shares in the victory of Christ. In Him he has power to tread on serpents and scorpions, and power to deliver and loose others from the bonds of the evil one."[70] A.B. Simpson explained the practical significance of this verse:

> It is not power that He gives us. We do not have the power. He has the power. But He gives us authority to act as if we had the power, and then He backs it up with His power. It is like the officer of the law stepping out before a mob and acting in the name of the government. His single word is stronger than a thousand men because he has authority, and

all the power of the government is behind him. So faith steps out in the name of heaven and expects God to stand by it.[71]

As believers we have authority to act as Christ's law enforcement officers, as legal authorities representing the government of the King.

Authority to Command in Faith. A.T. Pierson taught, "Obedience to Him means command over others; in proportion as we are subject to Him, even the demons are subject to us in His name."[72] A.B. Simpson explains this authority of faith: "Faith steps out to act with the authority of God's Word, seeing no sign of the promised power, but believing and acting as if it were real. As it speaks the word of authority and command, and puts its foot without fear upon the head of its conquered foes, lo, their power is disarmed, and all the forces of the heavenly world are there to make the victory complete." To Simpson, this was the secret of Christ's power, therefore the secret of our power as well:

> He spoke with authority, prayed with authority, commanded with authority, and the power followed. The reason we do not see more power is because we do not claim the authority Christ has given us. The adversary has no power over us if we do not fear him, but the moment we acknowledge his power, he becomes all that we believe him to be. He is only a braggart if we will dare to defy him, but our unbelief clothes him with an omnipotence he does not rightly possess. God has given us the right to claim deliverance over all his attacks, but we must step out and put our foot upon his neck as Joshua taught the children of Israel to put their feet upon the necks of the conquered Canaanites, and faith will find our adversaries as weak as we believe them to be. Let us claim the authority and the victory of faith for all that Christ has purchased and promised for our bodies, our spirits, or His work.[73]

Authority to Influence World Events. Throne Life understands that the believer's authority can exercise influence in world events.

MacMillan stressed this amazing truth that as we follow the urges of our spirit and take to the throne of God what He puts on our heart, we become "a partner with his Lord in the government of the universe." As we intercede, our prayers "become channels along which the divine power is enabled to flow for the alleviation of suffering, the extension of the gospel, and the control of the activities of the rulers of mankind." At our word, "the unseen principalities and powers are restrained, wars are hindered or delayed, calamities are averted, and national and individual blessings are bestowed."

Further, MacMillan declared, "Devastating wars might at times be held back if the Church of Christ realized its authority and privilege." He cited examples: "Even in world matters where war seemed inevitable, there have been times in recent years, when groups of instructed believers, united with one accord against the working of the powers of the air in some great crisis, have seen the problem gradually clear up without coming to the worst. Christians are far from realizing the extent and the reality of their union with Christ in His great task of world authority." Welsh intercessor Rees Howells is an example of one who practiced this with remarkable practical results before and during World War II.

Authority Over Depression. Depression often (though not always) comes as an attack of Satan. When attacked by depression MacMillan counseled himself to prevail with "a more positive attitude of resistance." Sarah Foulkes Moore relates a situation in which "a Christian worker was often conscious of a stupefying power coming over his mind and paralyzing his will. He was often pressed down and perplexed. He did not know of the oppression of the evil spirits in the atmosphere and did not resist the attacks, but stood passive and helpless before them. One day it came to him from God to say out loud, 'This is the devil. I resist him in the name and power of the Lord who conquered him at the cross.' He felt instant relief from the oppression on mind and body. His mind cleared. His will became strong to resist. His faith in Calvary's victory extricated him from a mass of perplexing circumstances that had, for years, hindered his testimony and prayer life."

Authority over Uncontrolled Anger. MacMillan recognized from his experience in ministry that "there is an intimate connection between sinful anger and the prince of evil, and sustained wrath will surely open the door to his entrance." One day MacMillan overheard two Christian workers, a husband and wife, arguing and yelling at one other. John and Isabel quietly, but firmly, took authority in the name of Jesus over the evil spirits behind the anger, commanding them to leave the couple. "Almost immediately," MacMillan remarked, "the quarreling stopped. As the authority was day-by-day held and renewed, the spirits were kept in check. Eventually however, the two separated, for they did not seek victory for themselves."

One of the Filipino Bible school students possessed a hot temper. "Stirred up by a trivial matter, he utterly lost control of himself, and speedily became almost insane with rage." MacMillan, as the head of the school, knelt in prayer in the room next to his, taking authority in the name of Jesus over the spirits of anger. In just a few minutes, the boy settled down, and the spirits that had incited him were subdued.

Authority over Excessive Fear. While traveling in a native boat among the islands off the coast of Mindanao, Philippines, MacMillan encountered a sizeable swell. His son Buchanan, who usually enjoyed sailing, suddenly was overcome with an uncontrollable fear that he had never had before in rough waters, and he cried to be taken ashore. MacMillan discerned that demonic forces were trying to stall the evangelistic effort, so he quietly claimed the authority of Christ over the spirits of fear and rebuked them, though saying nothing openly. In a very few minutes his son seemed to change completely, and for the remainder of the journey, lasting several days, there was no further difficulty. When they encountered a heavy squall a few nights later, in the midst of real danger with waves washing over the boat, his son had no fear.

On several other occasions, MacMillan encountered older, experienced missionaries with irrational fears. He again rebuked spirits of fear in the name of Jesus, resulting in dramatic changes. In one of those situations, a woman on a boat trip became highly agitated and began manifesting demonic symptoms. MacMillan again quietly exercised authority, binding the spirit in the name of Jesus Christ. The woman became still and the attack did not return.

Authority over Lying Dispositions. Sarah Foulkes Moore relates the story of a mother who "was grieved with the lying disposition of her child. Learning of the authority of 'His name'–quietly but firmly in the name of Jesus she rebuked the lying spirits and saw her child delivered."

Authority over Addictions. Through MacMillan's ministry God displayed amazing power in setting people free from addictive habits. A teacher at the Boys' School caught a young man chewing tobacco and sent him to MacMillan. The boy told him, "I cannot give it up, sir; I have tried again and again, and have failed." MacMillan responded, "Do you really desire to do so? The Lord Jesus is able to give you grace for victory." After counseling him further, they knelt to pray. MacMillan pled for him in prayer, and the boy "himself then took hold simply of the Lord."

Several weeks later MacMillan visited the young man and asked, "Are you having victory over the tobacco?" He replied, "I have not had a single taste for the tobacco since the day we prayed together in your office." MacMillan summarized the mighty work of God: "Thus God, in lands where the weed has been so widespread that practically everyone has used it, is Himself purifying and blessing the lives and bodies of His saved ones."[74]

Authority to Open Locked Doors to Evangelism and Missions. Sarah Foulkes Moore explains that we often encounter difficulty in evangelistic efforts with certain people because "the mind of the seeker after salvation seems bound and blinded." In her experience, "A quiet attitude of victory over the opposing spirits often brings quick deliverance of the captive."

From his experiences in China and the Philippines, MacMillan recognized that the forces of Satan often impede the advance of the gospel and must be rebuked: "The enemy has been preternaturally active; he has shut the doors of the lands against the Church's efforts; he presses on her heels as she goes forward. It is a time for those, who know the experience of sitting in heavenly places with the risen Lord, to hold the rod of His authority over the blocked roads before His people that all hindrances may be removed, that the way to the last tribes may be opened and the last individuals of the people for His name may be called out." MacMillan describes demonic obstacles to his evangelistic work in the Philippines:

> Here are hindrances to advance in the field work. . . . Ignorance binds the heathen mind in darkness that seems impenetrable. . . . Dissensions rise in the ranks of brethren, and the Spirit of peace withdraws. Behind every such situation the presence of the same malign powers can be assumed. The solution is in their displacement—we alone are to blame that they continue in power.

> The same principle is often applicable in personal evangelism. A soul under conviction has great difficulty in grasping the truth, or in yielding to it. His mind is blinded and bound. A quiet attitude of victory over the opposing spirits has often brought swift release. A Filipino student was suspected of lying, but was resolutely standing by his falsehood. Quietly the position was taken: "In the name of the Lord, I rebuke these lying spirits." Suddenly the student broke down, confessed, and wept his way through to victory.[75]

I could share many more such illustrations, but you get the picture of the authority we have in Christ. This authority is not exercised by only special, anointed people, but is available to every consecrated believer. You too can exercise authority over such hindering spirits, and trigger spiritual breakthroughs.

The Authority of Throne Influence—
The Magnetic Drawing Power of Christ

Sometimes we do not even need to exercise the authority of the Throne of God. Sometimes, just because of our position on the Throne and our exaltation of Jesus Christ, we are in a place of "Throne Influence." Jesus declared, "And I, if I be lifted up from the earth, will draw all men to Myself" (John 12:32). When we lift up Jesus, the magnetic drawing power of Jesus flows through us authoritatively. We have significant influence because others are attracted to Jesus within us. When they come in contact with us, they come in contact with Jesus within us.

As mentioned in Chapter 1, F.B. Meyer noted that to come into contact with God is to encounter a magnetic force that pulls us up to a higher dimension of living. When we touch Jesus, we become magnetized. We operate in the authority of throne influence and people are changed—not by us, but by the presence of Jesus within us. Let us pray as Meyer prayed:

Oh, let me touch You!
Let me dwell in unbroken contact with You,
that out of You successive tides of Divine energy
may pass out into and through my emptied and eager spirit,
flowing, but never ebbing,
and lifting me into a life of blessed ministry."[76]

For Reflection

1. How can we exercise the authority of the believers for binding and loosing?

2. In which of these areas mentioned above do you need to exercise authority and gain victory?

CHAPTER 6

Throne Experience—
The Enjoyed
Presence of God

"I pray that the eyes of your heart may be enlightened, so that you will know. . ." (Eph 1:18)

Paul's prayer is not that we would intellectually know in our mind. Rather, it is that we may experience. The word Paul uses for "know" means to know by experience, by acquaintance. Paul is praying that we might experience the hope of His calling, the riches of His inheritance in our lives and the surpassing power of resurrection life. So we can personalize Paul's prayer in Ephesians 3:16-19:

> Father of our Lord Jesus Christ, grant me, according to the riches of Your glory, to be invigorated with might through Your Spirit in my inner being, that Christ may dwell in my heart through faith, that I, being rooted and grounded in love, may be able to grasp with all the saints the width and length and depth and height—to know by experience the love of Christ that surpasses knowledge; that I may be filled with all the fullness of God.

If we are seated in heavenly places with Christ positionally, then positionally and legally we have everything in Christ. Positionally and legally, we are healed. Positionally and legally, we have victory. Positionally and legally, we have everything provided for that we need. Positionally and legally, we have every blessing in the heavenly places. It is a matter of making what is positional and legal then also experiential. As we more and more realize our position, we can more and more actualize our position—live it out experientially in our lives.

Throne Life Actualized

Andrew Murray declared, "The more a man lives in heaven, the better fitted he is to live on earth." Throne position is intended to become throne experience. It is not merely theological or academic. It is not abstract and ethereal; it is meant to be experienced. George Peck explains that throne-experience occurs "when the believer's enlightened faith successfully claims his associated position and privileges with Christ." The Holy Spirit imparts "to us a consciousness of union with Christ (John 14:20; 1 John 4:13), . . . whereby we realize that we are 'complete in Him which is the Head of all principality and power' (Col 2:10)." In other words, the Holy Spirit enlightens us.

Throne Experience Feels Vibrancy of Life. According to Peck, we have actualized Throne Life, or made it real, when our "association with Christ in heavenly places becomes vivid and habitual" and our "experience grows correspondingly victorious." He mentions three qualities of throne experience. First, our intimate connection with Jesus becomes "vivid." We have an "ah-hah!" experience in which we see clearly, brightly, vividly. We really envision ourselves in the presence of Christ. It is no longer just an abstract thought; we see Jesus like we have never seen Him before.

Throne Experience Becomes Habitual. Secondly, Peck explains that our association with Jesus is "habitual." It is abiding with Christ, staying in close contact with Him. No longer going up and down, back and forth, in the Holiest of Holies and out, but rather a consistency and a constancy of communion with Christ. When something becomes habitual, it becomes second-nature. We don't have to think about it. When we have actualized Throne Life, it becomes natural. We become naturally supernatural and supernaturally natural.

Throne Experience Is Victorious Life. Third, throne experience becomes a life of victory. It is then, Watchman Nee describes, "When eyes are really opened to see Christ as our victorious Lord, then our praise flows forth freely and without restraint. . . . Praise that is the outcome of effort has a laboured and discordant note, but praise that wells up spontaneously from hearts at rest in Him has always a pure, sweet tone."[77]

Throne Experience Is Throne Worship. Throne worship is not being worshipped at the throne, but worshiping at the throne. It means that all the while we are enjoying the privileges of Throne Life and exercising the authority of Throne Life, we are at the same time humbling ourselves before the one who sits on the throne. Even though we are coheirs with Christ and seated on the throne with Christ, we are not worshipped, but rather, we worship. We worship the head. Seated on the throne we are beneath the Head, submitted to the head, therefore we worship the head. Isaiah experienced such throne worship: "I saw the Lord sitting on a throne, lofty and exalted, with the train of His robe filling the temple" (Isa 6:1).

Throne Experience Delights in God's Presence. Tozer calls this throne experience, "The interior journey of the soul from the wilds of sin into the enjoyed Presence of God." He explains:

Though the worshipper had enjoyed so much, still he had not yet entered the Presence of God. Another veil separated from the Holy of Holies where above the mercy seat dwelt the very God Himself in awful and glorious manifestation. . . . It was this last veil which was rent when our Lord gave up the ghost on Calvary, and the sacred writer explains that this rending of the veil opened the way for every worshipper in the world to come by the new and living way straight into the divine Presence. . . . Ransomed men need no longer pause in fear to enter the Holy of Holies. God wills that we should push on into his presence and live our whole life there. This is to be known to us in conscious experience. It is more than a doctrine to be held, it is a life to be enjoyed every moment of every day.[78]

Tozer invites us, as ransomed people of God, to realize that we can live in the Divine Presence of Almighty God! Not just visit, mind you, but LIVE in His presence. This is what the old monk Brother Lawrence called "Practicing the Presence of God." We abide in His presence in the heavenlies moment-by-moment, day-by-day. Daniel Whittle expresses this thought well in his 19th century hymn:

> Moment by moment I'm kept in His love;
> Moment by moment I've life from above;
> Looking to Jesus till glory doth shine;
> Moment by moment, O Lord, I am Thine.

Life from above—moment-by-moment—this is throne experience, gaining our life, our strength, our enablement day-by-day by being connected to the Vine—by having the life of Jesus flow through us.

Throne Fellowship with the Trinity

Throne experience is real communion or fellowship with all three members of the Trinity—Father, Son, and Holy Spirit.

Abba Father—Intimacy with God. To many of us, God the Father is like a stern old man difficult to get to know, distant from us. The concept of God as the "numinous," the "wholly other," though true, often keeps us from realizing that God is not only transcendent, awesome and fearful, but that He is also personable, approachable, and desires a close personal intimate relationship and fellowship with

Him. A.W. Tozer calls that intimacy of the Holiest "the sacred gift of seeing, the ability to peer beyond the veil and gaze with astonished wonder upon the beauties and mysteries of things holy and eternal."[79]

Fanny Crosby understood personally that throne intimacy with God, relating it in her classic hymns "Draw Me Nearer" and "Blessed Assurance":

"O the pure delight of a single hour that before Thy throne I spend. When I kneel in prayer, and with Thee, my God, I commune as friend with friend."

"Perfect submission, perfect delight, visions of rapture now burst on my sight. Angels descending, bring from above, echoes of mercy, and whispers of love."

Abiding in Christ. A.B. Simpson opens the door of revelation into the throne room of God's presence through abiding with Christ:

You cannot receive the touch of life from the Living One unless your spirit and life are in touch with Him. The Christian who is taking things easy and not more than half out of the world will find it hard in the hour of need to establish connections with the life currents from above. . . . There is a "heavenly place" where we must walk with Him habitually and inseparably, if we would live the supernatural life and know the power of His resurrection in our bodies and the miracles of His Providence in answered prayer and victorious power.[80]

I thought I had understood abiding in Christ, but when I went through cancer, I learned to abide in Christ on a whole new level. I had to learn to walk with Jesus habitually and inseparably when I went through cancer. It was then I had the supernatural power to overcome.

Taught and Led by the Spirit. Throne experience is life in the Spirit. Paul tells us, "For the law of the Spirit of life in Christ Jesus has set you free from the law of sin and death" (Rom 8:2). As mentioned earlier, A.B. Simpson explains, "It is not so much the expulsion of sin, as the incoming of the Holy Spirit, which has broken the control which sin formerly exercised, lifting me into an entirely new sphere of holy life and victory." When we are in communion with the Holy Spirit, we are lifted to the heights. Paul goes on in the same chapter to say, "The mind set on the Spirit is life and peace" (Rom 8:6). Throne experience is enjoying life and peace in God's presence.

Paul continues, "For all who are being led by the Spirit of God, these are sons of God" (Rom 8:14). The word Paul uses here for "sons" means mature adult sons of God, not just children of God. In fact, the Apostle John, in his writings, never uses that term for believers, only for Jesus, the fully adult, mature Son of God. Yet Paul uses the term to indicate that when we are being led by the Spirit of God, we arise into a heavenly state of mature adulthood in Christ. This does not mean that we have become perfect, or rise to equality with Jesus as the Son of God, but rather that as we are led by the Spirit, we receive the privileges of mature adulthood in Christ.

Throne Experience Beholds God's Beauty and Glory. Bernard of Clairvaux in his sermon on the Song of Solomon describes the life experiencing the beauty and glory of the throne, the dwelling place of God, and bids us to seek it:

> Therefore the man who longs for God does not cease to seek these three things, righteousness, judgment, and the place where the Bridegroom dwells in glory: the path in which he walks, the wariness with which he walks, and the home to which he walks. About this home the Prophet says: "One thing have I asked of the Lord, that will I seek after: that I may dwell in the house of the Lord;" and again: "O Lord, I love the beauty of your house, and the place where your glory dwells." Of the remaining two he says: "Righteousness and judgment are the preparation of your throne." The man who is in earnest rightly seeks these three things, since they are the throne of God and the preparation of his throne.

When we seek righteousness, justice, and the presence of the Lord, we experience the beauty and glory of the throne of God.

Several years ago, my wife Kathy and I experienced glimpses of the beauty and glory of God's throne. We were driving through the Ozark mountains in Arkansas on our way to a pastor's retreat, we were listening to a worship CD by Michael W. Smith. As we reached the mountain top and our breath was taken away by the beautiful misty vistas of the valleys below, the song reached its climax of worship with the words "Holy, holy, holy." Simultaneously, a hawk was circling above us in perfect rhythm with the song.

We were transported into the heavenlies! We experienced a giddiness, light-headedness, and the awesome presence of God, so real and powerful that words cannot express it. My wife remarked that this was the first time she had experienced anything like holy laughter. We experienced the throne heights of the Holy of Holies for about ten minutes. What beauty! What glory! What rapture!

Throne Experience Produces Revelation. When we are at the throne of God, His Word becomes more alive to us. We can see Him and hear Him more clearly. A.B. Simpson assures us, "The Lord Jesus still gives His people hours of vision and revelation when they are elevated above the clouds and shadows of the present and permitted to come into closer touch with eternal things."[81]

Amy Carmichael illustrates hearing from the King at the throne of God: "When reading your Bible, have you not often noticed that some word has shone out in a new, direct, clear way to you? It is as though you had never read it before. You cannot explain the fresh vividness, the life, in it, the extraordinary way it has leapt to your eye—your heart. . . . You were in the very presence of your King at that moment. He was speaking to you. His word was spirit and life." Charles Spurgeon likewise portrays receiving a word from God at the throne:

You pray but have not the liberty you desire. A definite promise is what you want. You try one and another of the inspired words, but they do not fit. You try again, and in due season a promise presents itself which seems to be made for the occasion; it fits exactly as a well made key fits the lock for which it was prepared. Having found the identical word of the Living God you hasten to plead it at the throne of grace. . . . The matter is ended; sorrow is turned to joy; prayer is heard.

Throne revelations are glimpses into the throne, deeper and higher insights from the Word. This does not mean receiving any revelation that supplements or supersedes the Word of God, but fuller insights—illumination of biblical truth—come alive. Such revelations are always submitted to the Word of God and will not be contrary to the Word of God.

Throne Experience Produces Healing. The throne of God is a place of health and healing. Sickness does not exist at the throne of God. When we experience God's throne, we experience His healing presence. A.W. Tozer writes of A.B. Simpson, who was on the verge of dying from a heart condition and nervous exhaustion:

One Friday afternoon he walked out under the open sky, painfully, slowly, for he was always weak and out of breath in those days. A path into a pine wood invited him like an open door into a cathedral. There on a carpet of soft pine needles, with a fallen log for an altar, while the wind through the trees played an organ voluntary, he knelt and sought the face of his God.

Suddenly the power of God came upon him. It seemed as if God Himself was beside him, around him, filling all the fragrant sanctuary with the glory of His presence. "Every fiber in my soul," he said afterwards, "was tingling with the sense of God's presence." Stretching his hands toward the green vaulted ceiling he took upon himself the vow that saved him from an early grave.[82]

This is throne experience—God beside us, all around us, filling us with the fragrance of His glory, "tingling with the sense of God's presence." It was in this throne experience that A.B. Simpson experienced the healing touch of the throne of God. So can you. If you are in need of a physical touch from God, enter into the throne room, seek His face, and experience His presence. His power and love and peace will surround you and enable you to overcome your weakness.

Throne Experience May Be Overpowering. Sometimes we become so overwhelmed with the manifest presence of God that our physical bodies cannot take it. A.B. Simpson relates his own experience in his diary, "I ventured to ask Him for a special token and soon after He did give it—a very mighty and continued resting of the Spirit down upon my body until it was almost overpowering. . . . One afternoon it seemed as if heaven was opened and I was permitted to see myself seated with Christ in the heavenlies within the veil."

Throne Experience Produces Unspeakable Joy. When we come to the throne room, we experience "joy unspeakable and full of glory." (1 Pet 1:8, KJV). We are transported into the ecstasies of the heavenly. Heaven is filled with joy and laughter and jubilation. Lutheran pastor L.H. Ziemer came into this throne experience when he was baptized with the Holy Spirit: "Oh, glorious rapture of the soul! I arose, shouted, and sang, and laughed in the Spirit until I cried for very joy as the flood-tide of God's grace rolled in over my soul again and again with purifying and cleansing power. I felt the holy fire of God burning in my soul. . . . The Lord Jesus Christ was baptizing me with the Holy Spirit according to His Word and power."[83]

For Mary Mullen, a missionary with the Christian and Missionary Alliance, this unspeakable joy was an "otherworldly" experience: "It seemed as if a strong hand passed like a fluttering dove from my head down, and was felt in every part of my being. This was followed by an unspeakable joy and holy laughter." . . . The joy of the Lord flooded my entire being, until it seemed I could not stay in this world."[84]

A.W. Tozer understood that Throne Life can lead us into the most jubilant of experiences. Holy laughter would break out in his revival meetings, as Dr. Thomas Moseley, the president of Nyack College reported:

> What prayers! What faith! What expectancy! What convic-
> tion! What groaning in the Spirit! What claiming of prom-
> ises! What heart-searching! What victory! God in His
> faithfulness and love could not help but fulfill His own
> precious promise : "Call unto me, and I will . . . show you
> great and mighty things, which you know not.". . . One young
> man, after the Spirit had filled and overflowed his soul, cried
> out with holy laughter, "It's too much! It's too much! I can't
> stand any more!"[85]

Some might call such emotional demonstrations fanaticism, but A.W. Tozer understood throne experience, and noted approvingly of such manifestations: "So worship is capable of running from the very simple to the most intense and sublime."[86]

Throne Attitudes Activate Throne Experience

One of the chief keys to experiencing Throne Life is having a heavenly attitude, an attitude befitting the throne of God. Our atti-tude determines our altitude. If our attitudes are noble we rise above our circumstances. Paul counsels us, "Set your minds on the things above, not on the things that are on the earth" (Col 3:2). A.B. Simpson challenges us to rise up to think nobly and to experience the life of the throne: "How we should dwell on high, above all low and groveling things, and bear the dignity of princes of heaven. . . . How unworthy to be living a life of discontent, strife and misery."[87]

Throne Thoughts Are Noble Thoughts. God says, "For as the heavens are higher than the earth, so are My ways higher than your ways and My thoughts than your thoughts" (Isa 55:9). We acknowledge that God's ways and thought are far above our ways and thoughts. Yet in Christ, we can begin to think the thoughts of God, not merely our lowly thoughts. Our way of thinking is elevated to God's way of thinking, so that we think the thoughts of God after Him. That is why Paul can say, "For who has known the mind of the Lord that he will instruct Him? But we have the mind of Christ" (1 Cor 2:16).

When we are transformed by the renewing of our mind, we take on a Divine Mind, Christ's mind. We begin to think like Jesus thinks. We think well—we think more clearly; we think more intelligently; we think more soundly; we think more highly; we think divine thoughts. Puritan philosopher Thomas Traherne declares, "To think well is to serve God in the Interior Court; to have a Mind composed of Divine Thoughts, and set in frame, to be like Him within."

We experience the Throne Life of the mind of Christ whenever we live out Paul's counsel to let our mind dwell on noble thoughts: "Finally, brethren, whatever is true, whatever is honorable, whatever is right, whatever is pure, whatever is lovely, whatever is of good repute, if there is any excellence, and if anything worthy of praise, dwell [think on] on these things" (Phil 4:8). The context in which Paul wrote these words is dealing with anxiety vs. peace and joy. We are lifted out of anxiety and distress into peace and joy whenever we think noble thoughts.

Angry thoughts, anxious thoughts, envious thoughts, resentful thoughts, lustful thoughts, selfish thoughts—these all pull us off the throne of God and down to the earth. Noble thoughts, excellent thoughts, joyful thoughts, peaceful thoughts, forgiving thoughts, giving thoughts—these are throne-worthy thoughts through which we can rise above the world.

Throne Thoughts Enhance Our Faith. Hudson Taylor counseled, "How then to have our faith increased? Only by thinking of all Jesus is and all He is for us: His life, His death, His work, He Himself as revealed to us in the Word to be the subject of our constant thoughts."[88] Oswald Chambers similarly exhorted, "Think of the things you are trying to have faith for! Stop thinking of them and think about your station in God through receiving Christ Jesus."[89] Notice what he advocates here. First, he tells us to think about the things we are attempting to believe for. Then he tells us to stop thinking about them, and to change the focus of our minds. Think about who we are in Christ and what we have in Christ. When we get the focus off things and put our mind on throne-worthy thoughts, we can be in a receptive mode. There is an altitude in our attitude that enables our faith to soar to the heights.

Throne Thoughts Propel Us into a Noble Life. A.B. Simpson beckons us to consider or reckon ourselves as nobility: "Our reckonings reflect themselves in our realities . . . let the Master teach us not so much to rise as to remember we are risen. . . . Our attitude will influence our aim. People live according to their standing. The highborn child of nobility carries in his bearing and his mien the consciousness of his noble descent, and so those who have their title to be on high, and are conscious of their high and heavenly rank, walk as children of the kingdom."[90]

Thomas Watson stirs us to this heavenly altitude through stilling our mind and our entire being before God:

> To be still with God is the most noble life. It is as much above the life of reason—as reason is above the life of a plant; the true Christian is like a star in the highest orb, he looks no lower than a crown. *Grace puts high thoughts, princely affections, a kind of heavenly ambition into the soul.* Grace raises a Christian above himself, it makes him as Caleb—a man of another spirit. He lives in the altitudes, his thoughts are lodged among angels, and the 'spirits of just men made perfect.' Is not this the most noble life—to be still with God? The philosophers compare the soul of man, to a bird mounting up with her wings in the air. Thus with the wings of grace, the soul flies aloft, and takes a prospect of heaven.

Are you thinking the thoughts of God? Noble thoughts? Heavenly Thoughts? Princely thoughts? Are you Caleb—a man or a woman of another spirit? Are your thoughts lodged among angels? Personalize Paul's words and raise your thoughts into the heavenlies: "Whatever things are honest, and just and noble, and of good report, if there is any excellence, anything worthy of praise, I will think on these things, I will set my mind on these things." Then you will experience life at the throne of God.

For Further Reflection

1. What throne experiences have you had? What impact have they had on your life?

2. What thoughts do you need to change in order to have noble thoughts? What thoughts keep you from living in the heavenlies?

CHAPTER 7

Throne Banquet—
Feasting at the Royal Table

"Would we have Christ's exhilarating presence in the Supper?"
—Thomas Watson

The Puritan leader Thomas Watson stirs us to experience with exhilaration the heavenly presence of Jesus in the Lord's Supper! Holy Communion should never be a mere ritual. I have found that every time I partake of Communion with expectation and anticipation, something special happens. I am swept into the Manifest Presence of God. It becomes a throne experience for me.

The great early church father Chrysostom pictured the Lord's Supper as feasting at the table of royalty: "Look, I entreat you, a royal table is set before you. Angels minister at that table. The King Himself is there. And do you stand gaping? Are your garments defiled, and yet you make no account of it? Or are they clean? Then fall down and partake!"[91]

God and Man at Table Are Sat Down

When Jesus became God in the flesh through His incarnation, He brought heaven to earth. When we partake of the Table of the Lord, He lifts the earthly to heaven. Dr. Robert Stamps, Methodist minister and former Oral Roberts University chaplain, poignantly describes the union of heaven and earth in the Eucharist in his song:

> Elders, martyrs, all are falling down
> Prophets, patriarchs are gathering 'round,
> what angels longed to see now man has found.
> God and man at table are sat down.[92]

When you commemorate the Lord's Supper, you get a glimpse of what it is to sit at the banqueting table of heaven during the Millennium. Each time you partake in faith, you can experience the Presence of the Heavenly One.

Puritan Thomas Brooks viewed the Lord's Supper as "a reciprocal exchange between Christ and a gracious soul. Communion is Jacob's ladder, where you have Christ sweetly descending down into the soul—and the soul by divine influences sweetly ascending up to Christ." He expressed its meaning poetically:

> Communion with God is . . .
> a shield upon land,
> an anchor at sea,
> a sword to defend you,
> a staff to support you,
> balm to heal you,
> a cordial to strengthen you.
>
> High communion with Christ
> will yield you *two heavens,*
> a heaven upon earth,
> and a heaven after death.[93]

Tasting of the Heavenly Powers

Thomas Watson's eyes were opened to the heavenlies, envisioning the Lord's Supper as "a repository and storehouse of celestial blessings. . . . All the sweet delicacies of heaven are served at this feast."[94] We have not realized the fullness of these delicacies of heaven and the extent of the celestial blessings. In his majestic hymn "O the Depth of Love Divine," Charles Wesley also gazes into the heavenly realms, singing of exploring the depths of God's love and grace in the table of the Lord:

> O the depth of love divine,
> the unfathomable grace!
> Who shall say how bread and wine
> God into us conveys!
> How the bread his flesh imparts,
> how the wine transmits his blood,
>   fills his faithful people's hearts
>   with all the life of God!

Charles Wesley bids us to become a heavenly choir that sings of the mystery of the power of Communion that "fills his faithful people's hearts with all the life of God!"

> Let the wisest mortals show
> how we the grace receive;
> feeble elements bestow
> a power not theirs to give.
> Who explains the wondrous way,
> how through these the virtue came?
> These the virtue did convey,
> yet still remain the same.

Notice that he is filled with wonder that by God's grace "feeble elements bestow a power not theirs to give." In other words, we cannot understand or explain how it is that God works through the

Lord's Supper, but we do know that He does work supernaturally and conveys virtue to us.

> How can spirits heavenward rise,
> by earthly matter fed,
> drink herewith divine supplies
> and eat immortal bread?
> Ask the Father's wisdom how:
> Christ who did the means ordain;
> angels round our altars bow
> to search it out, in vain.

Here Wesley ponders how we can arise into the heavenlies and partake spiritually of "divine supplies and eat immortal bread," virtues we receive all the while being fed with the earthly elements of bread and wine. He does not pretend to understand nor does he try to figure it out intellectually and theologically, but acknowledges that even the angels do not understand.

> Sure and real is the grace,
> the manner be unknown;
> only meet us in thy ways
> and perfect us in one.
> Let us taste the heavenly powers,
> Lord, we ask for nothing more.
> Thine to bless,' tis only ours
> to wonder and adore.

Wesley understands that God's grace is conveyed in some mysterious, but real and certain, ways—God's ways. He bids us, "Let us taste the heavenly powers." What are some of those "heavenly powers," those "divine supplies"?

Heavenly Manna—Caught Up to the Third Heaven. Andrew Murray's daughter described about an occasion in which her father experienced being caught up to the third heaven while partaking of the Lord's Supper:

Can one ever forget the times when 500 or 600 communicants would gather around the Lord's Table, and the holy influence of the Lord that permeated the church? Can we forget the holy awe, the deep reverence, the joy and often the rapture written on father's face when "Heaven came down our souls to meet"?

I remember once that father seemed to have really been taken up to the third heaven and such a deep solemnity rested on us all before he spoke again with the words, "I live, yet not I, but Christ liveth in me, and that life which I now live in the flesh, I live in *faith*, the faith which is in the Son of God who loved me and gave himself for me." More especially father emphasized those words "who loved me." Oh the wonder of it that we so little understand! Let us love Him and trust Him more and more!

We left the Table feeling that we had indeed been fed on heavenly manna, and rose with a deeper love and fuller determination to do and dare all for our adorable Lord and Master. We were strengthened and refreshed as with new wine, and in the Thanksgiving Service afterward there was a time of wondrous praise, not from the lips alone, but from the heart.

A Heavenly Transfusion—Raised Up to More Than You Can Be. Thomas Watson declares, "Christ's blood has an elevating power, it puts vivacity into us, making us quick and lively in our motions." In a similar manner, Paul Brand, M.D., pictures partaking of the Table of the Lord as a heavenly transfusion: "When we come to the table we come with light breath, a weakened pulse. . . . We muddle along with our weaknesses, our repeated failings, our unconquerable sins, our aches and pains. In that condition, bruised and pale, we are beckoned by Christ to His table to celebrate life. We experience the gracious flow of His forgiveness and love and healing—a murmur to us that we are accepted and made alive, transfused."[95]

Brand intimates that when we drink of the Communion cup, it is as if Jesus is saying to us, "This is My blood, which has been strengthened and prepared for you. This was My life which was lived for you and can now be shared by you. I was tired, frustrated, tempted, abandoned; tomorrow you may feel tired, frustrated, tempted, or abandoned. When you do, you may use My strength and share My Spirit. I have overcome the world for you."[96]

Brand compares ingesting of the Communion juice to receiving a blood transfusion that infuses with fresh life and cleans toxins out of our bodies, involving "furious intercellular warfare . . . and the climactic effect of a serum injection on that struggle."[97] Thomas Watson, referring to Cyprian's description of persecuted Christians, says, "They arose up from the Lord's table, as lions breathing forth the fire of heavenly courage."

An ancient hymn from the sixth-century Communion Liturgy of St. James recognized the overcoming power of the Lord's Supper in a hymn that proclaims, "in the body and the blood—He will give to all the faithful His own self for heavenly food." He then goes on to say that as a result the angelic host of heaven provides protection and Christ, the Light of lights descends "that the powers of hell may vanish as the darkness clears away."

Heavenly Medicine from the Throne. When I was taking radiation and chemotherapy for rectal cancer in 2007, I discovered from the early church fathers that the Communion elements of bread and juice were considered "God's medicine for the soul." Bernard of Clairvaux declared, "The body of Christ is medicine to the sick." A.B. Simpson counsels that we can receive renewed energy and healing: "The Lord's very strength is given to you in this blessed communion. . . . get from Him His literal strength, physical quickening which fills our material being with new strength and sends us forth refreshed and enabled for the burdens and pressures and even the infirmities of life."[98]

So each night before I went to bed, I took the medicine prescribed by my Heavenly Physician. It was a little bit of heaven in the midst of the hell I was experiencing. As I record in my book *God's Healing Arsenal*, Communion was a part of the weaponry God led me to use for the healing of my body. I encourage you to make it a regular part of your weaponry too.

Divine Illumination at the Throne Banquet. On the day of Jesus' resurrection, as he walked with two of His disciples on the road to Emmaus, they did not recognize Him until He broke bread with them. Then their eyes were opened in partaking with Jesus. Simpson declares of the Lord's Supper, "Thus He gives to us His own very life in this blessed communion, to our spirit new life, to our mind new clearness of illumination, so that we can grasp, understand and realize the truth and realities of the hidden life, and to our body His own new life."

Heavenly Delights at the Throne Banquet. Right participation, with right motives and a heart made pure before God can bring about healing, fuller life, and blessing. I have personally known of several people who were healed or received other supernatural spiritual gifts, such as praying in tongues and prophetic words while receiving the Lord's Supper. A.W. Tozer tells of a man experiencing extreme joy while partaking of Communion: "I once saw a man kneel at an altar, taking Communion. Suddenly he broke into holy laughter. This man laughed until he wrapped his arms around himself as if he was afraid he would burst just out of sheer delight in the presence of Almighty God."[99]

A Feast of Freedom. Lloyd John Oglivie describes the Lord's Supper as a "feast of freedom," showing us that our eyes can be opened through Communion to see the liberty we have in Christ:

This is what it means for me to break the bread and take the cup. It means laying aside my prison garb to dine with the King. It means that I am set free to be the man God created me to be. To live life as it was meant to be lived. . . . I now invite you to this incredible feast of freedom.

What is it that binds you and keeps you from being a free man or a free woman? What memories of the past, what relationships of the present, what uncertainties of the future keep you bound? What cycle of condemnation are you locked into? What inflexibility, what habit patterns keep you incarcerated in the prison of life? Why is it that you react in certain situations the way you do and find it so difficult to grow to be the liberated, unique person you were meant to be?

The living Christ moves among us, and our bound and imprisoned spirits are suddenly lifted. He takes hold of us, lifts us up. Tenderly we see him face to face![100]

Prophetically, Oglivie writes further of being set free to dine at the King's Table, with the King of Kings Himself: "It is by grace that we come to this Table. To those of us who would cower at the sight of the banquet hall, who fear to come to the table, let alone stand with the kings, he says, 'Friend, come up higher. Come sit with me for I have released you from your own prison. I love you. I want you to be a free person.'"[101]

Come Up Higher and Feast Often!

Thomas Watson encourages us to partake of the Lord's Supper as often as we can, because "The more we take of the Bread of Life, the healthier we are." A.B. Simpson encourages us: "You can take Him for a month of life for your physical frame and you can enter into covenant with Him as your Physician for the days before you . . . to be your Guide, Master and spiritual supply for every need, and this blessed communion service may be to you an impartation of all that the body of Christ stands for—life, strength, health, fullness of supply for every need of spirit, soul and body."[102]

For Reflection

1. What does the Lord's Supper mean to you?

2. Have you ever experienced the presence of Jesus in a special way while partaking of Communion? What was it like?

CHAPTER 8

Throne Prayer

"Therefore He is able also to save forever those who draw near to God through Him, since He always lives to make interces-sion for them. For it was fitting for us to have such a high priest, holy, innocent, undefiled, separated from sinners and exalted above the heavens" (Heb 7:25-26).

Sometimes it feels like our prayers are like what was described in Deuteronomy: "The heaven that is over your head shall be bronze" (28:23). At such times it seems that our prayers are just hitting the ceiling and never reaching heaven. That happens when it is our own efforts at prayer, and we are not praying from our throne position. When we pray in weak human ways, we cannot touch heaven.

Throne prayer begins with Jesus, not us. The author of Hebrews tells us that He is at the right hand of the throne of God interceding for us before we ever pray a single prayer (Heb 7:25-26; 8:1; 12:2). Throne prayer means, first of all, that Jesus is praying for us and with us, and then through us. A.B. Simpson explains: "What does throne life mean for us His people? It means all the power of His interces-sion and priesthood. He is there as our Mediator. He is there to keep open every moment the fountains of prayer between us and the

Father. He is there as the One whom the Father hears always. And His effectual intercession secures for us the answer to our prayers and the acceptance of our persons continually before the throne."[103]

Entering the Palace of the King in Prayer

Chrysostom pictured entering the inner chamber in prayer (Matt 6:6) as a palace: "When you pray, it is as if you were entering into a palace—not a palace on earth, but far more awesome, a palace in heaven. When you enter there, you do so with complete attentiveness and fitting respect. For in the houses of kings all turmoil is set aside, and silence reigns. Yet here you are being joined by choirs of angels. You are in communion with archangels and singing with the seraphim, who sing with great aware their spiritual hymns and sacred songs to God, the Lord of all."[104]

John MacMillan recounts that "President Chiang-Kai-shek [of China] spent an hour in prayer each morning. . . .When the President went to his prayer room, he dressed himself in his robes of state, saying that he was having an audience with the King of kings, and it was becoming to render Him due honor."[105] We too have an audience with the King of kings!

Throne Intercession

As Jesus intercedes for us and we are seated with Him as His body, He then is also interceding through us. As we pray, not from the earth, but from our position on the throne in the heavenlies, our prayers become powerful and effective.

Throne Prayer Is the Spirit Praying Through Us. Paul exhorts us to "pray at all times in the Spirit" (Eph 6:18). To be in the Spirit is, first of all, to be in the spiritual realm, that is, to be in the heavenlies. So to pray in the Spirit means that we are praying in the spiritual realm of the heavenly places.

Second, to pray in the Spirit means to pray in a manner guided by the Holy Spirit. Throne prayer is not praying out of ourselves, but through the Holy Spirit.

Third, one type of praying in the Spirit is praying with the spirit, that is supernaturally with our human spirit initiated by the Holy Spirit. This is praying in the language of the Holy Spirit—praying in tongues. The chapter on "Throne Utterance" describes this kind of praying further.

Throne Intercession Emboldens Us. Andrew Murray gives us a glimpse into the Throne Life of prayer, "Here in union with Christ, in His unceasing intercession, we are emboldened to take our place as intercessors, who can have power with God and prevail." Throne intercession is done with confidence, not with doubts or weakness.

Throne Prayer Produces Answered Prayer. Jesus promises, "If you abide in Me, and My words abide in you, ask whatever you wish, and it will be done for you" (John 15:7). Throne Life is abiding in Christ. Andrew Murray explains that this state of abiding in Christ is when our prayers can be answered: "Faith as a spiritual act depends on the words abiding in us as living power . . . . Abiding in Christ is the place for receiving answers."[106] When we do not touch Jesus, our prayers are not answered; when we touch Jesus, the power flows to activate the answer.

At the Throne Divine Energy Is Released in Prayer. God's throne is a place of divine energy. John MacMillan writes about releasing divine energy from the throne of God: "As earnest, humble and continuous supplication is presented before the Throne, the divine energy is released, and flows forth in gracious streams of heavenly loving kindness."[107] As we pray from our position in Christ on the throne, divine energy flows from us.

We Advance the Kingdom through Intercession. John MacMillan grasped this concept perhaps more than any other, bidding us to advance the Kingdom through intercession:

Authoritative intercessors are men and women whose eyes have been opened to the full knowledge of their place in Christ. To them the Word of God has become a battle chart on which is detailed the plan of campaign of the Captain of the Hosts of the Lord. They realize that they have been appointed by Him for the oversight of certain sections of the advance, and they have accepted His commission. Deeply conscious of their own personal unworthiness and insufficiency, they yet believe God's statement concerning their identification with Christ in His throne power.[108]

The Prayer Closet Is the Command Post. John MacMillan describes the authority of intercessors:

Increasingly they realize that heavenly responsibility rests upon them for the carrying out of the warfare with which they have been charged. Their closet becomes a counsel chamber from which spiritual commands go forth concerning matters widely varied in character and separated in place. As they speak the word God obeys. His delight is in such co-working.

They have caught His thought concerning the method of the advance of His kingdom. Through them He finds it possible to carry forward purposes and to fulfill promises which have been long held back for lack not of financial means nor of human laborers-but of understanding spiritual fellow laborers.[109]

Our Hand on the Throne Prevails. In his book *Bridehood Saints*, George D. Watson wrote a chapter entitled "The Hand on the Throne," commenting on Moses lifting up his hands in intercession as the Israelites were battling the Amalekites (Exodus 17): "Because of the hand that was on the throne, that is, because the hands of Moses were held up in prayer, and those hands were laid on the throne of Jehovah and prevailed with God in getting the victory. . . . the Amalekites were conquered because the hands of a man were upon the throne."

He likens the action of Moses to the intercession of Jesus, declaring with authority, "It is because the hands of the man Christ Jesus are on the throne that His prayer prevails, and through Him we lift up our hands and place them on the same throne, that we may prevail against all our enemies. . . . And when we, like Moses, lift up our hands and through Jesus lay them on the throne of grace, it is then we gain the day."

Throne Prayer Wields the Rod of God in Our Hand. Elaborating on Watson's application of Exodus 17, John MacMillan explains the authority we have by wielding the staff of God through our intercession: "The rod [of Moses] symbolizes the authority of God committed to human hands. By it the holder is made a co-ruler with his Lord, sharing His throne-power and reigning with Him. . . . So today, every consecrated hand that lifts the rod of the authority of the Lord against the unseen powers of darkness is directing the throne-power of Christ against Satan and his hosts in a battle that will last until 'the going down of the sun.'"[110]

Throne Prayer Is Authoritative Over the Powers of the Air. MacMillan declared, like Watson, that the believer can assert "in prayer the power of the Ascended Lord, and the believer's throne union with Him. . . . Where in faith the obedient saint claims his throne-rights in Christ, and boldly asserts his authority, the powers of the air will recognize and obey."[111] Through our identification with Christ, seated with Him on His throne, when we speak with confidence from the throne, it is Christ speaking through us. The powers of the air will obey us as they would obey Christ.

Throne Prayer Is Coercing the Universe. Charles Spurgeon, the great Baptist preacher, grasped this principle of our authority in prayer, boldly proclaiming, "Prayer . . . is coercing the universe, binding the laws of God themselves in fetters, constraining the High and Holy One to listen to the will of His poor but favoured creature-man."[112] Spurgeon, a strong advocate of the sovereignty of God, nonetheless recognized the importance of our role in prayer: "On the throne of grace, sovereignty has placed itself under bonds of love.

God will do as He wills, but on the mercy seat, He is under bonds of His own making, for He has entered into covenant with Christ, and so into covenant with His chosen."[113]

It is important to understand that this does not mean coercing God. A.B. Simpson avows that "God is bound to act by our faith and our unbelief."[114] By this, however, Simpson is not saying that God is held hostage, but that God in His sovereignty has established this law by which He works and has voluntarily limited Himself to these laws, which are, in fact, a part of His nature. He explained, "Our Lord has announced this as the principle of His throne of grace, the law on which petitions will receive attention and consideration."[115]

Throne Prayer Is Establishing the Kingdom of God by Force. "From the days of John the Baptist until now, the kingdom of heaven has been forcefully advancing, and forceful men lay hold of it" (Matt 11:12, NIV). Throne Life is not received passively. It is taken forcefully. We must assert our authority in Christ.

Spurgeon recognized the believer's authority expressed in this verse: "You may force your way through anything with the leverage of prayers. . . . The kingdom of heaven still suffers violence and the violent take it by force. Take care that you work away with the mighty implement of prayer, and nothing can stand against you."[116]

A.T. Pierson, Spurgeon's interim successor, similarly affirmed, "No more wonderful fact confronts us in our actual experience of contact with this universe of God than the power He has given to man of commanding and controlling these eternal forces. They all move in obedience to certain conditions or in certain channels or modes of activity, which we call 'laws.'"[117]

Throne Declaration

". . . That the manifold wisdom of God might now be made known through the church to the rulers and the authorities in the heavenly places. This was in accordance with the

eternal purpose which He carried out in Christ Jesus our Lord" (Eph 3:10-11).

One type of throne prayer is "Throne Declaration," not merely praying for God's kingdom to come and His will to be done, but declaring to the powers of heaven and earth the will of the King. The word "made known" means to reveal by declaration. Some mistakenly presume to command principalities and powers. Scripture never demonstrates direct command of the highest powers of the heavens. In fact, John Paul Jackson, in his book, *Needless Casualties of War,* warns that such commanding puts us out of our league, and has many times resulted in spiritual attack, because we were never meant to attack the principalities in that way (see Chapter 10 on the dangers of Throne Life).

However, it is fully scriptural and appropriate to declare the truths of the mystery and wisdom of God to the powers. Paul tells us in Ephesians of the ways we can declare the wisdom and mysteries of God.

We Declare God's Wisdom Through Worship. We declare and reveal wisdom in the principalities and powers in the heavenly places, first of all, by our *worship*. The phrase "to the praise of His glory" is declared by Paul three times to the Ephesian church (Eph 1:5, 11-14). Declaring that we, as God's church, are the praise of His glory, reveals the wisdom of God. Worship is worth-ship—giving God His worth. When we are to the praise of God's glory, God's worth and wisdom are exhibited.

Even more, just a few verses after Paul writes that the church is to declare the wisdom of God to the principalities and powers, he makes a declaration of the glory and power of God: "Now to Him who is able to do far more abundantly beyond all that we ask or think, according to the power that works within us, to Him be the glory in the church and in Christ Jesus to all generations forever and ever" (Eph 3:20-21). When we make this declaration, God's wisdom is made evident.

We Declare God's Wisdom through Words. We declare to the powers by our words. We first declare God's wisdom by praying for wisdom and enlightenment (Eph 1:16-19).

Secondly, we declare the Word of God. Jesus assures us of the power of His Word: "The words that I have spoken to you are spirit and are life" (John 6:63). God promises, "So will My word which goes forth from My mouth; it will not return to Me empty, without accomplishing what I desire, and without succeeding in the matter for which I sent it" (Isa 55:11). Power is released in confessing and claiming the Word of God.

Third, we declare the purpose of God to the principalities and powers. John MacMillan explains, "The Church is to be God's instrument in declaring to these rebellious and now usurping powers the divine purpose."[118] Further, we declare God's wisdom by speaking the truth in love (Eph 4:15), by speaking wholesome words (Eph 4:29), and by singing psalms, hymns, spiritual songs (Eph 5:19).

We Declare God's Wisdom By Our Walk. Paul tells us in Ephesians 4 and 5 that we declare God's wisdom by walking worthy of our calling (4:1). We manifest God's wisdom by not walking like the Gentiles in futility of mind (4:17). We demonstrate God's wisdom by walking in love (5:2). We radiate God's wisdom by walking as children of the light (5:8). We exemplify God's wisdom by walking wisely and redeeming the time (5:15-16).

Commanding "Thy Kingdom Come"—
Your Decrees Are God's Decrees

"Pray, then, in this way . . . Your Kingdom come, Your will be done on earth as it is in heaven" (Matt 6:10).

Jesus told us how to pray. The Lord's Prayer is not merely a prayer we are supposed to recite repeatedly, but it is a model of how to pray. Jesus did not say, "Pray this prayer," but rather, "Pray in this manner. . ." It is a *way* of praying. "Our Father who is in heaven, hallowed be

Your name" takes us to the throne. By declaring the names of God, God is "enthroned on the praises" of His people (Ps 22:2).

To pray "Your Kingdom come, Your will be done on earth as it is in heaven," is a throne prayer—to bring God's rule and reign—God's throne—to earth. In Greek, the imperative is used of the verbs here, and thus can be translated, "Come Your Kingdom; be done Your will." There is a commanding force in the wording. Charles Spurgeon boldly asserts the power and authority of this prayer:

> Thou art thyself a decree. . . . Our prayers are God's decrees in another shape. . . . Do not say, "How can my prayers affect the decrees?" They cannot, except in so much as your prayers are decrees, and that as they come out, every prayer that is inspired of the Holy Ghost unto your soul is as omnipotent and eternal as that decree which said, "Let there be light and there was light." . . . The ear of God Himself shall listen, and the hand of God Himself shall yield to thy will. God bids thee cry, "Thy will be done," and thy will shall be done. When thou canst plead His promise, then thy will is His will.[119]

Throne Kingdom—Bringing Heaven to Earth

The kingdom of heaven is a Jewish idiom for the kingdom of God. We are seated in the heavenly places—in the kingdom of heaven. Where there is a kingdom, there is a throne. The kingdom of God is the domain of the King. Therefore, Throne Life is kingdom life. Life seated at the right hand of God with Christ in the heavenly places is life in the kingdom. Characteristics of kingdom life are the characteristics of Throne Life.

Throne Decrees Are Characterized by Righteousness, Peace and Joy. "For the kingdom of God is not eating and drinking, but righteousness and peace and joy in the Holy Spirit" (Rom 14:17). These are not self-centered decrees, but Christ-character-centered decrees.

When we decree from the throne, righteousness is established. Peace and joy abound.

Throne Decrees Activate Life in the Spirit. "The kingdom of God is . . . *in the Holy Spirit*" (Rom 14:17). When we are walking in the Spirit, we are walking on the heights. Where the kingdom of God is, the Spirit is in action. From creation, the Holy Spirit has always been moving: "The Spirit of God was moving over the surface of the waters" (Gen 1:2). The Spirit is dynamic, not static. If the Spirit is not moving, the kingdom of God has not come. Throne Life is not experienced. Throne Life is abundant, animated. When the Spirit is moving, animated, abundant life occurs. When we decree from the throne, the Spirit moves in power.

Throne Decrees Express the Will of the Throne. "Your kingdom come, Your *will* be done on earth as it is in heaven." The will of God is synonymous with the coming of the kingdom of God. It is God's will for His kingdom to come on earth. When we decree with commanding authority for God's will to be done, God's will indeed will be done.

Throne Decrees Claim with Confidence. Like Spurgeon, A.B. Simpson asserts our authority to claim: "In the name of Jesus we are to not only ask, but claim and pass in the orders of faith to the bank of heaven."[120] He noted that scholars had translated John 15:7, "You shall ask what you command and it shall be done unto you." He calls this "the confidence of prayer."[121]

Throne Decrees Command from the Throne. God Himself proclaims, "Ask me of things to come concerning my sons, and concerning the work of my hands command ye me" (Isa 45:11, KJV). E.M. Bounds calls this verse, "God's *carte blanche* to prayer."[122] Referring to the faith expressed in the appeal of the Syrophoenician woman, Bounds explains, "Jesus Christ surrenders Himself to the importunity of a great faith."[123]

Spurgeon's friend, A.T. Pierson likewise echoes: "Faith in God so unites to God that it passes beyond the privilege of asking to the power of commanding. This language of Christ is not that of a request, however bold, but of a *fiat*. . . . And so—marvelous fact! The child of God, laying hold by faith of the Power of the Omnipotent One, issues his fiat. . . . Obey the Law of the Power and the Power obeys you. Conform to the Laws and modes of the Spirit's operations, and in the work of God's hands you may command the Spirit's Power."[124]

We want to make clear that we are not commanding God; we are commanding what He decrees, and then He acts according to our confessions. We do not control God, but He does respond to our powerful proclamations of His purposes.

Throne prayer, then, is not merely prayer that comes from our mind, our desires, our thoughts, but prayer that is initiated and invigorated by the Holy Spirit from the very throne of God. It is not earthly prayer, but heavenly prayer, prayer conducted from the heavenly places, with heavenly words of authority and power.

Realize your position on the throne and pray with authority and power!

For Reflection

1. How can you enter the throne room in prayer? What keeps you from throne prayer?

2. About what circumstances in your life do you need to pray "Your kingdom come; Your will be done?" Pray those words over your circumstances right now.

CHAPTER 9

Throne Wilderness

"Then Jesus was led up by the Spirit into the wilderness to be tempted by the devil" (Matt 4:1).

As you read this chapter title, you may be thinking, "This is an oxymoron, a contradiction in terms. Wilderness is the antithesis of Throne Life." However, in God's kingdom things are upside-down and inside-out from the world's way of thinking. Wilderness experiences, which often involve great trials, are a part of Throne Life.

Throne Life is entered through trials and trouble: "Through many tribulations we must enter the kingdom of God" (Acts 14:22). Many people assume we receive Throne Life on a silver platter. Paul assures us, however, that kingdom life is only experienced through much trial and pressure.

Led Higher—To the Wilderness.

Being led higher is not always what we expect, not always what we are looking for nor would even desire. Consider the experience of Jesus after His baptism by John the Baptist in the Jordan River: "Then Jesus was *led up* by the Spirit into the wilderness to be tempted by the devil." The Greek word for "led up," *anago*, means "to lead up into a higher place." Geographically, Jesus went from the Jordan River to the deserts of Judea, which were at a higher elevation.

However, the Spirit did not lead Jesus upward geographically only, but spiritually as well. The Spirit of God was leading Jesus higher, but not to a place of exaltation. The Spirit led Him up to a place of desolation and temptation in order to experience the higher elevations of the overcoming life. Desert and desolation are part of the journey upward to the heights of God. The wilderness is a boot camp to prepare us for the battles for the Promised Land.

Spiritually, we want to be led higher, but do we want to be led higher into a wilderness? The journey to a higher life includes deserts, wilderness experiences. We do not think of wilderness experiences as highlights. We think of them as valleys. Yet often the wildernesses take us to a higher plane in the Christian life. The wilderness experience of Jesus raised him to heights of victory over the devil. The devil offered Him a shortcut to the throne, but He became enthroned by refusing the devil's throne.

If you drive westward through Kansas to Colorado on Interstate 70, you will find long stretches of flatland and little else. It is a long-g-g-g-g drive across the state. When you cross over into Colorado, the prairie land often seems even more desolate. There is even a town in Eastern Colorado called "Last Chance!" However, something you may not notice as you are driving across the eastern plains of Colorado is that you are gradually getting higher in elevation. When you reach Denver, you may not realize it, but you have arrived in the "Mile High City," at the brink of the foothills of the majestic Rocky Mountains. You did not take a steep mountain drive to get 5280 feet above sea level. You got there gradually, imperceptibly, over a long stretch of road. And before you is the gateway to the misty, majestic mountain passes! If you keep going westward toward the front range of the Rocky Mountains, you will pass through the city of Golden, Colorado, named for the famous gold rushes. In the autumn season, you will also see the beautiful golden color of the leaves of the aspen trees.

The journey to the highest mountains is through the arid desert lands. If we get weary, trial and temptation can pull us down into a pit. However, God intends that trial and temptation carry us to the highlands, the golden places, of the Christian life.

Cast Out into the Desert

Even more fascinating about Jesus' journey into the desert is reading Mark's account of the Spirit's leading: "Immediately the Spirit *impelled* Him to go out into the wilderness" (Mark 1:12). The Greek word for "impelled" is *ekballo*, meaning to expel, throw out, cast out." It is the same word used of casting out demons—a strongly forceful word. The Spirit of God thrust Him out into the wilderness to be tempted by the devil.

Early in my ministry, I felt cast out by God into the wilderness. I pastored a church in a tiny town on the semi-arid prairies of Eastern Colorado, like I described above. It sure did not seem like a pastoral advancement to me. I was a northeastern intellectual in a Colorado cowboy town. I really felt out of place and desolate. The old folk song "Home on the Range" came out of the very area where I was living:

> Home, home on the range,
> Where the deer and the antelope play,
> Where seldom is heard
> A discouraging word,
> And the sky is not cloudy all day.

Yes, I enjoyed watching the deer and the antelope play. And seldom did we see clouds in the sky, except when we had two feet of snow. However, I did not enjoy the atmosphere of the town, and I paraphrased the words, singing instead, "where seldom is heard an encouraging word, and life is all cloudy all day." In fact, at one point

I nearly had a nervous breakdown and received Christian counseling for six months.

In the midst of my difficult experience, God was working on my attitude and character. He was changing me from glory to glory (2 Cor 3:18)—away from my own pitiful glory into His holy glory. I now know that I could not have experienced a higher Christian life without having gone through that desert. God was taking me higher all along. I just could not perceive it. Imperceptibly, He was gradually increasing my spiritual elevation, preparing me for the majestic mountains of the heavenly life.

Surviving and Thriving in Our Wildernesses Day-by-Day

How do we survive our wilderness experiences? How do we thrive in Throne Life in our deserts? One who has walked that path, J. Furman Miller, counsels us:

> Although Throne Life is once for all provided for the believer the very instant he is born again of the Spirit, he must nevertheless learn to administer that which God has so graciously given. It is here that many fail and turn back. We are, through the virtue of our Savior, born again into heavenly places, with Him upon His throne; but we are still held responsible for our bodily life here upon the earth. To be fortified against breakdowns we must go all the way. We must not only assume a position in Christ, but we must learn to administer and control through the Holy Spirit our own body here upon the earth. The believer has two lives to live; one on the earth and another in heaven—and yet they are one. [125]

Daily Appropriation by Faith. Miller affirms that "All power over sin, self, sickness, and even Satan himself, is ours through the cross of Christ. It waits only the appropriation of faith. We need only believe, which means that we need only identify ourselves completely with Christ. . . . Faith is identification with Christ: He with us, we with Him. It begins at the Cross as the sinner sees Jesus dying in his place and identifies that God-killing sin as his own. He cries out, 'That sin is mine; that Cross is the cross of my sinfulness; that death is the death I deserve.' Thus he identifies himself with Jesus on the Cross and in the Savior dies beneath the wrath of God's just penalty for his sin."

Receive Overcoming Strength for Each Day—One Day at a Time. Miller recognizes that we still have to live life here on earth; our theology, however sound and lofty it may be, still has to be worked out and proven in our life. He understands that some may be saying, "This all sounds very good, but it is far too wonderful for human ears; what has all this heavenly rhapsody to do with my personal problem which daily keeps threatening the breakdown of my faith?"

Therefore, Miller gives some practical biblical counsel for receiving overcoming strength for each day, one day at a time, "As your days, so shall your strength be." As the old country song goes, "One day at a time, sweet Jesus." When we grasp and accept this we will receive "that overcoming strength which awaits all enthroned ones."

Four Daily Prescriptions. Miller urges believers "to translate every provision of the Throne Life into terms of twenty-four hour periods and to experience personally the difference such a way of thinking and trusting makes." In order to make it through our desert experiences, Miller gives four daily Throne Life prescriptions to appropriate "the fullness of power and blessing of the enthroned life," based upon God's plan for the Israelites in the wilderness after their exodus from Egypt:

* ✶ *Daily Diet of Manna from Heaven*—Feed on the Word of God as Our Daily Bread. "This strength which God so freely provides must be received early in the morning, feeding on the Word with Jesus on His Throne. . . . They are commanded by

the sovereign Physician, whose name is Jehovah-Rapha: 'I am the God who heals you.'"

★ *Daily Exercises for Forgiveness of Sin and Consecration.* The daily sacrificial offerings remind us "that just as we must have proper exercise in addition to proper food, if we wish to be healthy, so we must exercise ourselves about our sinful condition in relation to the perfect will of God for our lives, if we wish to have strength. The entire redemptive work of Jesus is built around this concept of the morning and evening sacrifice. . . . Each unit of our eternal lives is intended by God to be surrounded by the offering of the blood of the Lamb without spot or blemish for the necessary cleansing from sin, plus the complete consecration of our lives to do His will. . . . we must reaffirm it every day. . . . We must exercise ourselves about Him every day."

★ *Daily Social Contacts of Love and Reconciliation.* "Life is much more than just eating and sleeping. We are gregarious beings who require social contacts. Here, too, the same principle holds, and for this need of our lives God has given the same promise: 'Let not the sun go down upon your wrath.' The unit is still the day, and our Creator knows very well that many breakdowns are the result of our harboring bitterness, anger, and unforgiveness in our hearts. God's method is the therapy of love."

★ *Daily Work—Don't Worry about Tomorrow.* We must never forget that wherever and for whatever we may be called, every sphere of service is attainable only by a day-by-day process. It is the quality of our preparation today, plus that of tomorrow (which has by then become another today), and so throughout all our days, which determines our life work for the Master. Undue concern about the future task results inevitably in discouragement and neglect; but this frequent cause of breakdown is arithmetically eliminated when one comes to realize that each today added to its neighbor, like beads on a string, eventually includes this future task. God never calls anyone to be a missionary three years from now; just for today."

These are four keys Miller advocates for living out Throne Life daily in our deserts—"God's prescription, His preventative grace against breakdowns." He exhorts us, "If we will thus learn to live the Throne Life as God intends. . . . May God now teach us so to number our days, one by one, from this today throughout every day of all our lives. May we thus each new day re-enter fully into the joy of the Lord, for the joy of the Lord is the strength of His people, and as your days so shall your strength be—enthroned and over all."[126]

For Reflection

1. What wildernesses have you experienced or are now experiencing? How is God leading you higher through your deserts?

2. Which of the four prescriptions are you lacking in order to make it through your wilderness? What can you do to put into practice those prescriptions?

CHAPTER 10

Throne Warfare—
The Dangers of Throne Life

"Put on the full armor of God, so that you will be able to stand firm against the schemes of the devil. For our struggle is not against flesh and blood, but against the rulers, against the powers, against the world-forces of this darkness, against the spiritual forces of wickedness in the heavenly places" *(Eph 6:11-12).*

Before we become too heady with the rights and privileges of Throne Life, we need to be aware that both godly and malevolent principalities and powers are also found in heavenly places. Spiritual warfare is part and parcel of Throne Life. MacMillan cautions, "The heavenlies . . . are also the place of most intense conflict. Let the believer, whose eyes have been opened to the comprehension of his throne rights in Christ, definitely accept his seat and begin to exercise the spiritual authority which it confers upon him. He quickly realizes that he is a marked man."[127]

Living Throne Life prepares us for warfare. If we are not living Throne Life, we get defeated. Throne Life does not prevent warfare and subtle deception, but it equips us to face it. Our enemy throws down many challenges to Throne Life.

Dangers of Throne Life

Sitting with Christ on the throne of God can be a heady experience. For if we do not maintain humility, we experience the dangers of Throne Life as well as the joys and the privileges. J. Furman Miller describes the necessary preparation for throne warfare: "If we would exercise our blood bought throne rights, if we would join in intercessory prayer for deliverance from captivity of those under the domination of Satan, if we would secure from the Giver of life health for the afflicted, if we ourselves would be free and well, we must meet the enemy with complete understanding of his method and with God's prescribed spiritual equipment." Oswald Chambers was a part of the Higher Life movement a century ago, yet he also warned against dangers of the movement, some of which we address below.

Danger of Deception. The higher you go in God the rarer the atmosphere. If you cease breathing in the life of God, you will become dizzy, light-headed. You may lose your bearings. The enemy becomes more subtle at these heights. After the victories in the Promised Land at Jericho and Ai, Joshua and the Israelites succumbed to subtle deception by the Gibeonites. So many times we have seen great men and women of God who have experienced God's glory and anointing fall prey to the subtle deception of Satanic forces. "Therefore let him who thinks he stands take heed that he does not fall," Paul warns (1 Cor 10:12).

You see, the heavens are not only God's territory, but also the territory of the unseen powers of darkness in the heavenly places. They use strategies and powers not known or understood on earth. If you are not wary, you will think you are in the Spirit. You indeed are in the realm of spirits, but not all that is in the spirit realm is of the Spirit, that is, of the Holy Spirit.

Danger of Exercising Energy of the Flesh. J. Furman Miller writes of the need for throne rest in the midst of activity to avoid over-zealous striving: "Successfully to wage our spiritual throne-warfare we must rest unreservedly in Christ's completed victory over all of Satan's forces on the Cross. Leave the fighting to Him, forsaking fleshly zeal for spiritual rest. Then labor ceaselessly to enter into that throne-rest from which all power flows. This is the only cure for sloth. The effort exercised is to the end that we be still and see the Lord perform, as we present our bodies to Him."[128]

Danger of Plateau or Complacency. If we enjoy our current status too much, we may just want to stay there, rather than pressing on for more of God. We become lukewarm or tepid. God does not like lukewarmness. He would rather that we be hot or cold (Rev 3:15-16). In our tepid state, He spits us out. If we are half-hearted, we lose the momentum to move on higher and further in God. When we overcome our apathy, we rise above ourselves to sit on the throne. Jesus promises, "He who overcomes, I will grant to him to sit down with Me on My throne, as I also overcame and sat down with My Father on His throne" (Rev 3:21).

Danger of Leaving Our Throne Position. Sarah Foulkes Moore cautions, "This ruling and overruling authority of the Lord is avail-able for us, if we are under the blood and full of the Holy Spirit. We can never employ this power in our own spirit. If, when dealing with the enemy, we give way to our own spirit it means sure defeat. In occupying the Throne-seat the enemy cannot attack. The enemy's strategy is to entice the believer from his position of authority and get him vexed, burdened, confused, depressed, or self-occupied. The seat of authority far above the enemy in union with Christ is the believer's security."

Kris Vallotton explains this for 21st century believers: "When our entire prayer life is motivated by the negative circumstances surrounding us, it is a symptom of our seating arrangement. Earthly seating creates reactionary prayers. If we sit there long enough, we will end up with a BIG DEVIL and a little God."[129]

Danger of Self on the Throne. Throne Life is the Christ life, not the self-life. We can forget that we are only on the throne as Christ is on the throne. We are on the throne in Him, not in our selves. We begin to view ourselves as something, as someone, rather than selves in Him. Oswald Chambers called it "Christ-esteem." Chambers cautions:

> When we are born again we enthrone Ishmael, that is, we consecrate our natural gifts and say these are the things with which God is going to do His work: they are the things God makes His servants, and I have to see that they are put in the position of servants. If I put them on the throne, I start a mutiny within my own soul. . . . It is the man who can rule his natural spirit that is able to take the city. It is only when we have learned to bring the natural life into perfect submission to the ruling personality of God that God dare turn His saints loose. It is of no use to turn out a lot of half-baked Ephraims into unlimited power. If I enthrone natural pride or natural virtue, I am in total insubordination to God in just that partic-ular and cannot be His son or daughter."[130]

Danger of Our Mind on the Throne. As we experience Throne Life, we find that God enlivens our minds to greater capacities than ever before. We experience deeper and higher understandings. We begin to claim, "I have the mind of Christ." However, we may fail to realize that Paul uses the plural, "<u>We</u> have the mind of Christ" (1 Cor 2:16), meaning that the church, the entire body of Christ, has the mind of Christ. Not any one person can say, "I fully, perfectly, have the mind of Christ." We begin to think we have great insights, and forget that it is God who has given us a heavenly mindset. As Oswald Chambers observes, "We enthrone common sense, and tack the name of God on it.[131] He warns against taking the initiative on our own and putting "our wits on the throne."[132]

On the other hand, some people's minds are so focused on spiri-tual matters, that they neglect the practical matters of life or relation-ships with other people. They become so heavenly-minded, that they are no earthly good. Watchman Nee cautions, "Unless we bring heavenliness into our dwellings and offices, our shops and kitchens, and practice it there, it will be without meaning."[133]

Danger of Pride—Throne Cockiness. Because we are God's royalty, we may begin to think that as a King's Kid, we are hot stuff. Watchman Nee again warns, "We make the mistake of thinking that we have already 'come of age'—that we are already mature sons." [134] This activates the danger of deception. As we deceive ourselves, we become more easily deceived.

Danger of an Entitlement Complex. Related to pride is a mentality of entitlement or elitism. We forget where we came from, and come to believe we are entitled to rights and privileges beyond our capability or authority to handle. Oswald Chambers gives the antidote to this, "We waive our rights to use our rights."

Danger of Throne Revelations. Others think they have a corner on the truth, a hotline to heaven, and get caught up in mystical speculation or deceitful philosophies. Paul warned about "taking his stand on visions he has seen, inflated without cause by his fleshly mind" (Col 2:18). This is the danger of Gnosticism, the belief that we have secret elite knowledge into the spiritual realm. We must never get to the place where we think we are more spiritual or have greater revelation because of our throne experiences. Oswald Chambers calls this "hole-and-corner aspect—secret times alone with God," in which our belief in our secret revelations can deceive us.[135] Chambers gives this sound counsel:

> If your experience is not worthy of the Risen, Ascended Christ, then fling it overboard. Whenever ecstasies or visions of God unfit us for practical life they are danger signals that the life is on the wrong track. Our identity with Jesus Christ is immediately practical or not at all; that is, the new identity must manifest itself in our mortal flesh otherwise we can easily hoax ourselves into delusions. . . . this spiritual anarchy based on *my* intuitions, *my* private interpretations,

my experiences, while refusing to submit to the words of the Lord Jesus.[136]

Danger of Misinterpreting Throne Revelations. We need to always keep in mind that even if we do receive a genuine revelation from God, we are but fallible transmitters of an infallible God. Higher Life writer May Mabette Anderson had great insight into this danger of misinterpreting a voice or vision from God:

> Beloved, let us understand and admit one for all, that we are exceedingly *fallible* creatures. So very *fallible*, in fact, that, though our Father may be very desirous of imparting to us some truth and though He may breathe into the soul in all His Divine purity, yet when we undertake to give it voice and pour it out in verbal phrase to others, we are more than apt— unless we lie low at His feet in deepest humility—to so tarnish and becloud it by our clumsy touch and exaggerated language, as will place it beyond the Divine recognition.

> A revelation may be truly from God. Yet, being such imperfect transmitters and interpreters of the Divine thought as is true of each one of us, one may easily be mistaken in the interpretation given to such revelation. Those who confidently aver that marvelous experiences have been given them, accompanied by visions and repeated assurance that a certain one who is ill has been already healed or is to be healed in the future, and then following such assurance the sick one dies without healing having been experienced—such persons either misinterpreted God's revelation, or have mistaken the voice of the Adversary for that of the Holy Spirit.[137]

Danger of Throne Glitter. Recognizing that we are royalty can cause us to focus on the glory and glitter of Throne Life. We have a sensational God, and sometimes He does sensational things. Sometimes we experience, in some tangible way, the glory cloud of His presence. However, if we put our attention on the sensational experience rather than the sensational Person, all we end up with is glitter rather than the real substance—which is the glory of God Himself.

Danger of Presumption. Some people assume that because we are children of the King, we can name and claim anything that we want. This is why Andrew Murray explains the difference between the *right* of inheritance and the *possession* of that inheritance: "The death of the testator gives the heir immediate right to the inheritance. And yet the heir, if he be a minor, does not enter into the possession. A term of years ends the stage of minority on earth, and he is no longer under guardians. In the spiritual life the state of pupilage ends, not with the expiry of years, but the moment the minor proves his fitness for being made free from the law, by accepting the liberty there is in Christ Jesus."[138] A believer can, therefore, only inherit what he or she is mature enough to handle.

Lest we think we can have it all here and now, we need to remember that the Kingdom of God is here now, but not fully here yet. We must recognize and acknowledge our limitations, but we do not succumb to them. We accept that we have limitations, but we must be careful not to increase our limitations by talking about how we are limited.

Danger of a Superman Mentality. This is related to the ancient heresy known as Gnosticism, the belief in a special secret revelation that is for the elite. Not all share in this level of power. This is a feeling that we have arrived. Oswald Chambers cautioned about "an amateur providence attitude" in which a believer becomes, "as it were, god almighty," thinking, "I am not likely to go wrong, but you are."[139] He especially warned, "The disposition of sin is not immorality or wrongdoing, but the disposition of self-realization—I am my own god. . . . It has the one basis, my claim to my right to myself."[140] Again Chambers cautions us against getting a big head: "We are not all excellent supermen."[141]

Danger of Satan's Elevation. Oswald Chambers cautions that Satan can take us to heights, but not God's heavenly heights:

The Golden rule in temptation is—Go higher. When you get higher up, you face other temptations and characteristics. Satan uses the strategy of elevation in temptation, and God does the same, but the effect is different. When the devil puts you into an elevated place, he causes you to fasten your idea of what holiness is far beyond what flesh and blood could ever bear or achieve. Your life becomes a spiritual acrobatic performance high atop a steeple. You cling to it, trying to maintain your balance and daring not to move. But when God elevates you by His grace into heavenly places, you find a vast plateau where you can move about with ease.[142]

Danger of Thinking We Are Invincible. If we are not properly putting on the full armor of God, and doing so with humility, the enemy can catch us off guard. Paul reminds us, "We have this treasure in earthen vessels. . . . but though our outer man is decaying, yet our inner man is being renewed day by day" (2 Cor 4:7a, 16b).

This kind of attack especially comes upon us after a spiritual peak experience or victory. After Elijah experienced the power of Throne Life in defeating the priests of Baal, he was threatened by Jezebel. Instead of maintaining his throne position, he became afraid and depressed.

Dangers of Strategic Level Spiritual Warfare. Some people in a popular movement today called "strategic level spiritual warfare" try to command territorial spirits and pull down strongholds in the heavenly places. Terry Law, an international minister who has served with Oral Roberts on the board of Oral Roberts University, warns, "Without realizing it, many of those who engage in 'pulling down' spirits today are really paying tribute to evil angels."[143]

In his book *Needless Casualties of War*, John Paul Jackson warns, "Unless you understand the parameters of our delegated authority and some practical guidelines on how to properly engage in spiritual warfare, there's a strong possibility that you could become an unfortunate victim of war."[144] He makes it clear that the scriptural boundaries of directly engaging the powers do not involve commanding spirits in the second and third heavens. We need to know what authority Christ has delegated to us and in what spheres.

Overcoming in Throne Warfare

Regard Satan as a Defeated Foe. Ruth Paxson writes that one of the chief marks "of life lived on the highest plane is—*it is an overcoming life*. Having taken his position by faith in the heavenlies in Christ the spiritual man lives in the atmosphere of triumph which prevails there. The spiritual man is on top of his difficulties; he is the conqueror not the conquered; the victor not the vanquished. His identification with Jesus Christ in the victory over sin and Satan is a reality to him and he looks upon Satan as an already defeated foe and treats him accordingly and reckons upon his own death to sin, to self and to the world."[145]

Declare the Power of the Blood. Sarah Foulkes Moore exhorts us to exercise our throne authority through the blood of Christ:

> The believer's refuge is *under the blood* of Jesus where no force or power of the enemy can penetrate. The cross has robbed Satan of his power. To overcome him, present the blood on the face of every attack from the pit whether the attack is upon the church, family, mind, soul, body or circumstances. Satan is overcome by the blood (Rev 12:11). Bind the blood upon him. It takes away all his abrogated authority and power. . . . The blood of Jesus is God's provision for overcoming the enemy. The blood of Jesus is the token of Christ's complete victory over Satan and his evil forces and their complete subjection to Him as He sits on His Throne. . . . By faith ask God to cover every part of your conscious and sub-conscious being with the blood of Jesus. Then say aloud, "Jesus' blood does *now* protect every part of me, and does *now* destroy the power of the devil." A definite stand in the authority of the

Lord must be taken, absolutely refusing to give place to the devil in whatever form he manifests himself in the church or home, in body, mind or spirit.

Exercise Spiritual Discernment. A.W. Tozer once declared that the gift of discernment was the gift most needed in the church today. We exercise spiritual discernment through:

* knowing and interpreting the Word of God properly (2 Tim 2:15).
* inspecting the fruit (Matt 7:15-23).
* testing the spirits (1 John 4:1-3; 1 Thess 5:19; 1 Cor 12:3).
* exercising the gift of discerning spirits (1 Cor 12:10).
* seeking out godly, wise counsel (Prov 11:14; 24:6).
* having our senses exercised through practice (Heb 5:14).

When we remain alert and actively seeking to discern the subtleties of spiritual warfare, we will not be taken off guard when the dangers and deceptions come.

Maintain Your Throne Authority in Warfare. Ultimately, our victory in times of throne warfare comes by staying alert from our vantage point on the throne, keeping dressed in our heavenly armor from the throne, and standing firm in our position at the throne: "Finally, be strong in the Lord and in the strength of His might. Put on the full armor of God, that you will be able to stand firm against the schemes of the devil" (Eph 6:10-11). This is what A.B. Simpson describes in his song "Living in the Glory":

> I have found a heaven below,
> I am living in the glory.
> Oh, the joy and strength I know,
> Living in the glory of the Lord.
>
> Storms of sorrow 'round me fall,
> But I'm living in the glory;

> I can sing above them all,
> Living in the glory of the Lord.

When we are maintaining the heavenly life in the midst of our earthly life, we can live in the glory of the Lord. Living in the glory does not mean absence of suffering or sorrow. Rather, it means singing above all the storms even while going through the storms. Simpson goes on to show that living in the glory also does not mean exemption from attack of evil powers:

> Satan cannot touch my heart
> While I'm living in the glory;
> This disarms each fiery dart,
> Living in the glory of the Lord.

Simpson acknowledges that the fiery darts *will* come. "Higher Ground," the old theme song of the Higher Life movement, expresses this same thought:

> I want to live above the world
> Tho' Satan's darts at me are hurled
> For faith has caught the joyful sound
> The song of saints on higher ground.

Even above the world in the heavenlies, Satan's darts are hurled. However, if we are living Throne Life, Satan cannot touch our heart. Even though the flaming arrows are flying all around us, and sometimes even seem to hit us, living Throne Life quenches the fiery darts, preventing them from doing permanent damage. Simpson declares further:

> I can triumph over pain
> While I'm living in the glory;
> I can count each loss a gain,
> Living in the glory of the Lord.

Again, Simpson avers, Throne Life does not mean a painless life. Rather, it means that we can endure and victoriously overcome pain. Every loss is not a permanent loss, but an ultimate gain, when we are living in the glory of Throne Life. Make this your confession in the midst of your throne warfare:

> Yes, I'm living in the glory
> As He promised in His Word.
> I am dwelling in the heavenlies,
> Living in the glory of the Lord!

For Reflection

1. In what ways are you experiencing throne warfare? How can you overcome?

2. What dangers of throne life do you perceive in your own life? How can you avoid those dangers?

CHAPTER 11

Throne Enduement— Power from the Throne

"Tarry in the city until you are clothed with power from on high" (Luke 24:49).

W e cannot live Throne Life without throne power—power not of our own, but power from on high. "On high" is a biblical idiom for heaven or the throne of a king. That power from on high in Luke 24:49 is further described by Jesus as power from the Holy Spirit: "You will receive power when the Holy Spirit has come upon you; and you shall be My witnesses both in Jerusalem, and in all Judea and Samaria, and even to the remotest part of the earth" (Acts 1:8).

Throne power is derived from our authority as a believer. There is an important principle here in understanding the dynamic inter-relationship between authority and power. Power without authority is illegitimate; authority without power is inadequate. So while we possess authority as believers, we also need to access the power of the throne—to be endued with power from on high.

Throne power can only be tapped into from the location of the throne—in the heavenly places. Jesus told His disciples, "It is to your advantage that I go away; for if I do not go away the Helper will not come to you; but if I go, I will send Him to you" (John 16:7). Jesus ascended to the throne to endue His disciples with power from the throne. Throne power is only obtained through Christ. It is for that reason Paul directs his praise to Jesus: "Now unto Him who is able to do far more abundantly beyond all that we ask or think [in the heavenly places] according to the power that works within us, to Him be the glory . . ." (Eph 3:20). It is not some New Age energy within ourselves that we tap into; it is power only from heaven, only from Jesus, only from being in covenant relationship with Him.

Pentecost Takes Us into the Throne Room

This enduement of power from on high historically came on the day of Pentecost, when heaven invaded earth, when the Holy of Holies descended and enveloped the disciples. As Andrew Murray, in his great commentary on Hebrews, *The Holiest of All*, explains, "It was on the day of Pentecost that they truly entered within the veil." When we experience our own personal Pentecost, we enter within the veil of the Holy of Holies, into the throne room of the King. Higher Life leaders like Murray, A.B. Simpson, and others called this the "sanctifying baptism in the Holy Spirit."

Throne Power Is the Elevator to the Higher Life. A.B. Simpson declared that the baptism in the Spirit is God's great elevator to the higher planes of the Christian life. He called it "God's great Elevated Railway, . . . borne along on His Ascension pathway by His own Almighty impulse. It is God's great Elevator, carrying us up to the higher chambers of His palace without our laborious efforts. . . . lifting us into a supernatural life."[146]

Years later Oswald Chambers echoed Simpson's insight, "by the baptism of the Holy Ghost, He can lift us into the heavenly places where He can reveal the counsels of God to us. . . . We can be lifted into such a relationship with the Father that we are at one with the sovereign will of God by our free choice, even as Jesus was."[147] These

Higher Life writers show us that we cannot reach throne heights without the baptism in the Spirit.

Enthronement Is Power Released. Edith Beyerle, a devotional writer of Throne Life, explains "His enthronement does not mean His absence. It rather means power released—all the throne power of Christ brought to bear upon other lives through our yielded lives."[148] Jesus spoke of that release of the Spirit, "From his innermost being will flow rivers of living water" (John 7:38). Classic writers like John Wesley often distinguished in this Scripture between *infusion* (the indwelling of the Holy Spirit at regeneration) and *effusion* (the subsequent outpouring or release of the Holy Spirit from within).

Puritan theologian John Howe described his throne experience of the outpouring of the Spirit upon him from on high as being "awakened from a ravishing and delightful dream . . . a wondrously copious stream of celestial rays from the lofty throne of the Divine majesty seem to dart into my open and expanded breast . . . far surpassed the most expressive words my thoughts can suggest. . . an inexpressibly pleasant melting of the heart. . . . tears gushing out of my eyes for joy." Have you experienced that release of the Spirit?

Enthronement Is Life Energized. Ruth Paxson writes, "The spiritually minded man has learned God's way of maintaining his life in the heavenlies and his life is energized by the mighty power of the Holy Spirit whom God bestows upon every child of His. The Holy Spirit is given when the new nature is imparted to the believer for the very purpose of effecting this growing conformity to the image of Christ. . . . Life on the highest plane is consistently and continuously maintained by the energizing power of the indwelling power of the indwelling Spirit of God."

Empowered to Live a Witness— A Holy, Transformed Life

Jesus promised that when we are endued with the Spirit of power from on high we would receive the power to be a witness of Himself.

That power to be a witness of Jesus manifests in three vital dimensions of our life:

- ★ power to *live* a witness—to live a holy and victorious life.
- ★ power to *speak* a witness—to speak with boldness, wisdom, anointing, and the leading of the Holy Spirit.
- ★ power to *demonstrate* a witness *supernaturally*—through signs and wonders, gifts and manifestations of the Spirit.

Evangelicals tend to emphasize the power to speak a witness. Holiness people tend to stress the power to live a witness. Charismatics and Pentecostals focus on the power to demonstrate a witness supernaturally. However, God intends that we be endued from on high with all three dimensions of power.

First of all, we receive the power from on high to live a witness— to live a holy, victorious witness of a life transformed by Jesus. This is often called the *sanctifying* baptism in the Holy Spirit, because He is, after all, the <u>Holy</u> Spirit—the Spirit of holiness. A.B. Simpson describes the glorious experience of entering into the throne room and becoming transformed through the experience of Pentecost:

- **The Holy Glory Penetrating Our Whole Being.** "Beautiful type of the work of sanctifying grace—the holy Shekinah of the divine Spirit and the indwelling Christ in the innermost chamber of the spirit, and spreading their heavenly life and influence abroad through every part until they penetrate every faculty of the soul and every organ of the physical being with their transforming and consecrating power."

- **Transfusion of the Life of God Within.** "When the tabernacle was finished the Holy Spirit came down and possessed it, and dwelt in a burning fire upon the ark of the covenant between the cherubim. God lived there after it was dedicated to Him. So when we are dedicated to God He comes to live in us and transfuses His life through all our being, . . . so that every movement, every thought, every intention, every desire of our whole being will be prompted by the springing life of God within."[149]

Throne Power Puts Us More in Touch with God's Thoughts. Throne power also elevates our mind into the heavenlies and transforms our thoughts. Simpson explains further, "When our whole physical being is permeated with the presence of God and the baptism of the Holy Spirit, we are in more distinct touch with God's thoughts, influence and suggestions."[150]

Throne Power Is the Key to Throne Victory. A.B. Simpson's friend and colleague A.J. Gordon understood throne enduement as the key to a victorious Christian life: "One may experience a great crisis in his spiritual life, in which there is such a total surrender to God and such an infilling of the Spirit, that he is freed from the bondage of sinful appetites and habits, and enabled to have constant victory over self instead of suffering constant defeat."[151]

Throne Power Expels Self and Desire for the Things of the World. A.B. Simpson declared, "If you get filled with God, there will be no room for you." Oswald J. Smith, pastor of the renowned People's Tabernacle in Toronto, described the power of holiness through the baptism in the Spirit: "You will be so filled with Him that you will not want the world. It will be the expulsive power of a new affection. The new will expel the old. You will find your greatest delight and joy in God's service, and you will discover that you are miserable and unhappy in the world."[152]

Throne Power Produces Increased Spiritual Benefits. Carrie Judd Montgomery shared the transforming power of the baptism in the Spirit in her own life: "There has been a great increase of holy joy. . . . an increased holy stillness, as all the powers of my being have been brought into subjection to the law of the Spirit of life in Christ Jesus. . . . a great increase of love. . . . increased power to witness, . . . increased teachableness, a willingness to learn from the humblest believer in Christ, ... increased love for the Word of God, and a glad yielding to its authority. . . . an increased spirit of praise."[153]

Empowered to Speak a Witness—A Transformed Tongue

When we are endued with power from the throne, our speech is transformed. We speak not merely our words, but words from the throne. Higher life scholar Dr. Ira David describes this transformation as "one that loosens all tongues and sets them all on fire for God at once."[154]

We receive power to speak a witness—to speak with anointing, boldness, wisdom, and the leading of the Holy Spirit.

Throne Enduement Empowers Us to Speak with Anointing from the Holy Spirit. A.B. Simpson explains, "It gives effectiveness to our message and convicts the world through us of sin, righteousness and judgment. It not only works in the preacher, giving unction and power to His message, but works distinctly in the heart of the hearer, producing divine impression, conviction, persuasion, faith, and salvation."

A.W. Tozer noted that even Jesus depended upon the anointing: "Even our Lord Jesus Christ ministering in the time of His humanity among us depended upon the anointing of the Spirit. . . . When leaders and members of a church do not have the genuine gifts of the Spirit—the true anointing of the Spirit—they are thrown back upon human and natural capabilities."[155]

F.F. Bosworth related the powerful anointing he received: "Since being baptized with the Holy Spirit I have seen greater results in one service than during eleven years between the time of my conversion and my baptism with the Holy Spirit."

Throne Enduement Empowers Us to Speak with Boldness. According to A.B. Simpson, the main purpose for the baptism in the Spirit "is to fit us for Christian service as witnesses for Christ. It gives personal courage, boldness and faith in witnessing for God and testifying to men. . . . It equips us for our special ministries as evangelists, teachers, rulers, comforters, pastors, helpers. . . . It is the spirit of revival coming down, not only upon individuals, but upon multitudes in mighty floods of Pentecostal blessing and leading men and women to cry, 'What must we do to be saved?'"[156]

Throne Enduement Empowers Us to Speak with Wisdom. A.B. Simpson explains, "It gives love for souls and holy tact and wisdom to win them. . . . It gives wisdom for the emergencies which we are called to meet. . . . It is the only power that can give energy, fervor, efficiency and glory to our work."

Throne Enduement Empowers to Intercede from Heaven. Simpson emphasized, "It is especially manifest in the ministry of intercession and becomes the spirit of intense prevailing prayer." For F.F. Bosworth, this was significant: "To me the greatest phase of the Baptism in the Spirit is the spontaneous life of intercession."[157] This was my own experience as well. After I was baptized in the Spirit, I had an insatiable hunger and thirst for prayer, and I would spend hours in intercession.

Throne Enduement Produces a Change in Our Speech. A.B. Simpson writes, "The baptism of the Holy Spirit is a baptism for our tongues, and if it does not bring us a new tongue it should bring us a new message, a new unction, a new mighty power, to be silent from the voices of earthly folly, clamor and sin, and charged with heavenly might to witness for Jesus Christ to the uttermost part of the earth."[158] Dr. Ira David asserts, "A proper baptism of the Holy Spirit will fix our tongues so that we shall stop saying the wrong things and begin to say the right."[159]

What these Higher Life writers are saying is that whether or not we speak in tongues when we are baptized in the Spirit, our tongues will be affected in some way. Our speech will change; our language will be filled with godly, anointed words.

Empowered to Demonstrate a Witness Supernaturally—Throne Gifts and Graces

The power we receive is a supernatural power. As A.B. Simpson stated above, the baptism in the Spirit is "lifting us into a supernatural life." The Higher Life is a supernatural life.

Supernatural power is demonstrated supernaturally, so we should expect supernatural demonstrations of God's power from the throne. Supernatural spiritual gifts are not given for merit; we cannot earn them. They are *charismata*, that is, "grace gifts," or "gracelets," as John Wimber called them. George Peck counsels, "It does not tend to edification to possess a spiritual gift without a corresponding grace." Throne gifts are throne graces, and throne graces accompany throne power.

Throne Enduement Bestows Gifts from the Throne. The ministry gifts in Ephesians 4:11 (apostles, prophets, evangelists, pastors, and teachers) are sometimes called "ascension gifts," because they were given by Christ upon His ascension. Ascension gifts come from the throne of God; they are rooted in the throne of God. They are, therefore, throne gifts. The Holy Spirit is our ascension gift from Christ.

On the day of Pentecost, Peter proclaimed that God raised Jesus to sit on His throne (Acts 2:30), and as a result "therefore being by the right hand exalted, and having received of the Father the promise of the Holy Spirit, He has shed forth this which you now see and hear" (Acts 2:33). The manifestations of the Spirit on the day of Pentecost (prophecy, speaking in tongues, wind, tongues of fire, etc.) were bestowed by Jesus from the throne of God. All of the gifts of the Spirit are thus throne gifts.

Throne gifts are not used for our glory, but for our edification and the edification of others. They are not for show; they are for showering the love of God upon others.

Spiritual Gifts Are the Full Equipment for Ministry. A.B. Simpson declared, "These are additions to our special enduement for service, and we are encouraged to 'covet earnestly the best gifts,' our full equipment for the ministry of Christ . . . an additional experience, or a special ministry."[160] William C. Stevens, an early dean of Nyack College, called the lack of miraculous gifts "incomplete effusions of the Holy Spirit," by which he meant outpourings of the Spirit that lack manifestations "which marked 'the early rain' demonstrations of gifts and powers in the Spirit."[161]

In other words, our throne enduement is incomplete without activating supernatural spiritual gifts through our lives. In fact, A.W. Tozer wrote that missing gifts are a "tragedy in the church."[162] More than a century ago, Charles Spurgeon anticipated the need for supernatural gifts to increase:

> If at the commencement of the gospel we see the Holy Spirit work great signs and wonders, may we not expect a continuance—if anything, an increased display—of His power as the ages roll on? . . . If there is not a miraculous spiritual power in the church of God today, the church is an imposter. . . . Only let men come back to the real gospel and preach it ardently, not with fancy words and polished speech, but as a burning heart compels them and as the Spirit of God teaches them to speak it; then will great signs and wonders be seen. We must have signs following; we cannot otherwise answer the world.[163]

All of these classic Higher Life advocates emphasized that we need a supernatural equipping for supernatural work. Throne Life requires throne equipment.

Ministering from the Throne

When we are empowered from the throne to live a witness, speak a witness, and demonstrate a witness supernaturally, we minister, not in our own strength, but in the strength, anointing, and illumination from the throne of God. We live out in our actions and experiences the prayer Jesus taught us to pray, "Thy Kingdom come, Thy will be done, on earth as it is in heaven." Heaven invades earth. Throne power is manifested through us on earth.

When We Minister from the Throne, We Receive a Tangible Manifestation of His Touch. A.B. Simpson experienced this in his anointing to pray for the sick, saying, "Dear friends, I never feel so near to the Lord . . . as when I stand with the Living Christ, to manifest His personal touch and resurrection power in the anointing of the sick."[164] He sensed the tangible manifest presence of God, because he was in touch with Jesus at His throne. The power of the Holy Spirit often flowed through him like an electrical current: "The effect of prayer and anointing is sometimes like an electrical shock in a mild form. . . . Many members of my congregation have experienced this aid in some form, often by a direct cure of some ailment, physical as well as spiritual."[165]

When We Minister from the Throne, Gifts Flow Fully and Freely Through Love. When throne power is manifested, supernatural gifts of the Spirit flow, gushing forth freely and fully in love. John MacMillan writes of this as "love's divine overflow": "Into their hearts is to be shed abroad by the Holy Spirit, the very love of God Himself, so that they shall love their brethren and the men of the world around with an affection that is supernatural. . . . How such a display on earth of the spirit of heaven would revolutionize the Church! False ambition would find no place. . . . The Holy Spirit, ungrieved by carnality, would be manifest in such power that His gifts would once again be in full exercise in the assembly, to the glory of God."[166]

When supernatural power is manifested from God's throne, the Spirit is not quenched, but is given full rein to move in power. At the same time, when power comes from God's throne, excess is quenched and the flesh is subdued. Divine love reigns.

When We Minister from the Throne, We May Receive a Divine Message from the Inner Chamber of God's Presence. A.E. Thompson wrote of A.B. Simpson's prophetic anointing, "The prophet . . . has come out of the inner chamber of God's presence with a specific message for a special occasion." He identified Simpson as among "the circle of those to whom are committed to the oracles of God." If we spend time at the throne, we receive the revelation of the throne to share with others. It is filtered through our fallible lips and therefore, not always pure in our communication, but it is a message from the heavenly throne.

When We Minister from the Throne, the Overpowering Glory of God May Flow into Us or Through Us. Higher Life pastor Mary Gainforth testified of the overwhelming glory of God in her life and ministry: "Since I have been consecrated to the work of the Lord and received the baptism of the Holy Spirit I have been prostrated under the power of God. At one time it seemed that my whole being was filled with the glory of God. Wave after wave passed over my soul until every thing seemed like a bright shining light. I could see nothing of this world and still I realized what was going on."[167]

Carrie Judd Montgomery described it as being weakened by a delightful weight of glory: "A 'weight of glory' rested upon my head, which I could distinctly feel, and even see in the Spirit. I was filled with joy and praise to God with an inward depth of satisfaction in Him which cannot be described. . . . I became weak physically under the greatness of the heavenly vision."[168]

Lest people think this is just some charismatic or Pentecostal emotionalism, Higher Life scholar Dr. T.J. McCrossan describes this power coming upon people as he prayed for them: "All who are genuinely under this power praise the Lord Jesus in a marvelous manner. Many of them have visions of their Lord in Heaven. Some see Him on the cross, and, praise God, many are baptized with the Holy Spirit before the Holy Spirit is through with them."[169] Church history is replete with examples of this power from the throne in the ministries of John Wesley, Jonathan Edwards, Charles Finney, Peter Cartwright, A.B. Simpson, Andrew Murray, and others.

When We Minister from the Throne, Divine Presence, Discernment, and Authority Flow through Us. DeVerne Fromke distinguishes between ministering *for* the Lord in the Outer Court from ministering *from* the Lord in the Holy of Holies, what he calls a "royal ministry of spiritual service" and "the ultimate ministry": "When we move out from the Lord, it is with a peculiar discernment, a unique authority, and an amazing contentment. Like Moses . . . we shall bear upon our faces the glory of the ONE we minister to others. Such a ministry is more than instrumental for God, it is EXPRESSIVE OF GOD. . . . People always recognize one who has lived in His presence, one who has experienced the crystal sea of Eternal Truth— God Himself. When such a one moves out to minister, his authority is not legal, but spiritual, his sacrifices are not symbols, but reality, he shares more than knowledge—he shares Christ."[170]

When We Minister from the Throne, We Do Not Struggle in Our Own Effort. Throne enduement means His divine energy flowing through us, not our ministering in our strength. We minister from a position of throne rest. Watchman Nee explains, "In relation to Him there is work to do, but it is work that produces no sweat (carnal energy)." A.B. Simpson captured this revelation in his timeless hymn "Himself":

Once it was the blessing, now it is the Lord;
Once it was the feeling, now it is His Word.
Once His gifts I wanted, now the Giver own;
Once I sought for healing, now Himself alone.

Once 'twas painful trying, now 'tis perfect trust;
Once a half salvation, now the uttermost.
Once 'twas ceaseless holding, now He holds me fast;
Once 'twas constant drifting, now my anchor's cast.

Once 'twas busy planning, now 'tis trustful prayer;
Once twas anxious caring, now He has the care.
Once 'twas what I wanted, now what Jesus says;
Once twas constant asking, now 'tis ceaseless praise.

Once it was my working, His it hence shall be;
Once I tried to use Him, now He uses me.
Once the power I wanted, now the Mighty One;
Once for self I labored, now for Him alone.

Once I hoped in Jesus, now I know He's mine.
Once my lamps were dying, now they brightly shine.
Once for death I waited, now His coming hail;
And my hopes are anchored, safe within the veil.

For Further Reflection

1. Of the three dimensions of the power of the Spirit, which is the most lacking or most needed in your life?

2. In what ways do you sense throne power flowing through you? Do you sense you are ministering from the throne?

CHAPTER 12

Throne Utterance— Tongues of Men and of Angels

"Tongues of men and of angels"(1 Cor 13:1).

". . . a very glorious and blessed channel of direct fellowship with the heavenly world, and in some sense a real opening of the doors between the earthly and the heavenly."
—A.B. Simpson

P raying in tongues is the language of heaven—language from the very throne of God. On the day of Pentecost following the outpouring of the Holy Spirit and speaking in tongues, Peter explained the miraculous occurrence: "This Jesus God raised up again, of which we are all witnesses. Therefore having been exalted to the right hand of God, and having received from the Father the promise of the Holy Spirit, he has poured forth this, which you both see and hear" (Acts 2:32-33).

Peter is saying that Jesus, at the right hand of God, poured out the Holy Spirit and the gift of tongues from the throne. From these verses we can observe:

* Speaking in tongues is given by Jesus.

* Speaking in tongues comes from the throne of God.

* Speaking in tongues is a result of the pouring out of the Holy Spirit from heaven.

* Therefore, tongues is "throne utterance"—utterance or language—a heavenly language from the very throne of God.

Prayer in tongues is utterance from the throne of heaven through the interior throne of the heart—with the spirit. Jesus empowers the human spirit to speak with the Divine Spirit—the Father in heaven. It is communicating from spirit to spirit, communing in spirit with the Father. Jack Hayford calls it "the beauty of spiritual language."

Praying in tongues is spiritual language from the throne of God. Paul speaks of praying in tongues as "the tongues of men and of angels." The supernatural language of the Spirit can be expressed as human languages supernaturally given or the ecstatic languages of heaven that are beyond human understanding. Praying in tongues is a way of communicating with heaven and of speaking the mysteries of heaven (1 Cor 14:2). When we all get to heaven, tongues will no longer be necessary because we will know and speak the language of heaven.

The Experience and Value of Throne Utterance[171]

Although the Apostle Paul emphasized the need to speak intelligibly in public church services, he testified that he spoke in tongues in his private prayer times more than anyone else. We know from his testimony that he prayed day and night—many hours of prayer. It is therefore likely that he spent many of those hours praying in tongues. Regardless of the misuses of tongues in the Corinthian church, he considered praying in tongues as valuable in his own life.

Paul affirmed that "One who speaks in tongues edifies himself" (1 Cor 14:4). Some who do not understand speaking in tongues have attempted to claim that this verse indicates a selfishness—edifying self, rather than others. If that were so, Paul would have been a very selfish man. Although some may have selfish motives for speaking in tongues, that is not what this verse means. Rather, it means edifying ourselves spiritually. The word "edify" in Scripture is always used in a positive sense. Regardless of how some people may misunderstand or misuse the gift of tongues, if speaking in tongues is given by Jesus, it must be good. If it comes from the throne of God, it must have a holy, beneficial purpose. Paul certainly thought so.

Let us consider the value of throne utterance, not from modern day Pentecostals or charismatics, but from the testimonies and teachings of respected classic Higher Life leaders who believed in the reality and value of speaking in tongues. Many of them experienced speaking in tongues themselves. Others, such as A.B. Simpson, may not have experienced tongues, but they attested to their worth by what they observed and heard from their close friends and associates who did experience such throne utterance.

Divine Ecstasy—Caught Up to the Throne of God. When a person prays in tongues, he or she is caught up to the throne of God. Although he apparently desired but never spoke in tongues, A.B. Simpson understood this from the experiences of his friends. He called it "the expression of divine emotion," explaining:

> It appears to be a divine ecstasy which lifts the soul above the ordinary modes and expressions of reason and utterance. . . . The spirit is the higher element and in the gift of tongues appears to overlap the mind altogether, and find its expression in speech quite unintelligible to the person himself and yet truly expressing the higher thought and feeling of the exalted spiritual state of the subject."

Carrie Judd Montgomery, A. B. Simpson's close friend, testified of this in her own experience: "In my private devotions, or with some friend of the same mind, I have been given sweet, ecstatic utterances which seemed indeed like the tongues of angels."

Heavenly Mysteries. From his own experience, the Apostle Paul explained, "For the one who speaks in a tongue does not speak to men, but to God; for no one understands, but in his spirit he speaks mysteries" (1 Cor 14:3). For Carrie Judd Montgomery, praying in tongues was expressing those heavenly mysteries: "A 'weight of glory' rested upon my head, which I could distinctly feel, and even see in the Spirit. I was filled with joy and praise to God with an inward depth of satisfaction in Him which cannot be described. To be thus controlled by the Spirit of God and to feel that He was speaking 'heavenly mysteries' through me was most delightful. The rivers of living water flowed through me and divine ecstasy filled my soul. I felt that I drank and used up the life and power as fast as it was poured in. I became weak physically under the greatness of the heavenly vision."

A Channel of Fellowship with the Heavenly World. If speaking in tongues is speaking to God in mysteries as Paul describes, then it is a heavenly means of communication. A.B. Simpson muses on the meaning of supernatural spiritual language: "[The Apostle Paul] recognizes [tongues] as the distinct mark of divine power and presence, and a very glorious and blessed channel of direct fellowship with the heavenly world, and in some sense a real opening of the doors between the earthly and the heavenly." Praying in tongues opens channels of divine communication, intimate communion with the heavenly.

Entering on Holy Ground. W. T. Dixon, Quaker missionary who served as a church-planting pastor in the Christian and Missionary Alliance expressed his throne experience of tongues as holy ground: "As we come to [this] class of tongues, let us take the shoes off our feet, for the ground whereon we stand is holy. . . . This is where the supernatural predominates to such a degree that God is more in evidence than man, or simply the operation of the Spirit upon man. It is a speaking manifestation of Deity—a supernatural Spirit-given utterance to men clothed with power and authority from on high."

Intensive Worship. Although there is no evidence that A.W. Tozer spoke in tongues, he had a high regard for tongues as an expression of intense worship of God: "When the Holy Spirit came on the day of Pentecost, why did the believers break out into ecstatic language? Simply, it was because they were rightly worshiping God for the first time. Intensive worship unexpectedly leaped out of their hearts."[172]

It Is the Residue—Like Icing on the Cake. Mrs. William T. MacArthur, wife of A.B. Simpson's close friend and associate, experienced speaking tongues at a camp meeting, and expressed it as an overflow of anointing: "This [Pentecostal baptism] was like the 'residue of the oil' (Lev 14:18, 26) that flowed down upon the hem of Aaron's robe, and that God was doing this thing for all who would receive." In other words, it is the icing on the cake that tops off one's spiritual experience.

Greater Consciousness of God's Presence—Beyond All Dreams. Bertha Pinkham Dixon, wife of W.T. Dixon, testified, "Out from my innermost being rolled a volume of language unknown to me, while my soul was filled with 'joy unspeakable and full of glory,' which found vent in this new operation of the Spirit. I was literally drunk with 'new wine.' This 'weight of glory' remained for days, while the consciousness of the divine presence within was greater than I had ever dreamed possible in this life."

Strengthening the Inner Man. William T. MacArthur, close associate of A.B. Simpson and father-in-law of actress Helen Hayes, testified of a divine inner strength: "It is being strengthened with might by His Spirit in the inner man. . . ." I found that inner strength and relief by praying in tongues while in pain after cancer surgery.

The Highest and Best of Our Heavenly Inheritance. William MacArthur again bears witness that "tongues are valuable . . . in proportion as the speaker communes with God. . . . It seems to us that it is not possible to reach the highest and best of our heavenly inheritance apart from them."

Greater Liberty and Divine Unction. Throne utterance produces liberty and boldness of spirit. Early Christian and Missionary Alliance pastor H.L. Blake extolled the value of throne utterance in his life: "I have far greater liberty and Divine unction on me in dealing with souls, and there has come into my life an overflow of love and joy with a deep settled peace planted in the depths of my soul, a something that is inexpressible and indescribable."

Expressing the Holy Spirit's Burden. A.B. Simpson understood tongues to be an expression of the unutterable groanings of the Holy Spirit: "It would seem as if in these last days God had sometimes to give a new tongue to adequately express the burdens of the Holy Spirit's prayer. Therefore, we cannot always expect to fully understand our own prayers, but must often pour out our hearts before Him in wordless agony and unutterable desire, knowing 'that He who searches the hearts knows the mind of the Spirit, because He makes intercession for the saints according to the will of God.'"

Five Benefits to Robert Jaffray. Robert Jaffray, a Higher Life Presbyterian Canadian who became missionary statesmen to Asia with the C&MA, was highly respected worldwide. He testified of his own experience of throne utterance: "Personally I have never received such a spiritual uplift as when I received this blessed Baptism and spoke in tongues. The anointing then received 'abides' unto this day." He mentioned a few of the many benefits he received from praying in tongues:

- ★ *Deeper Love and Understanding of the Word of God.* "A deeper love for, and understanding of, the Word of God than ever before."

- ★ *A Sense of Our Powerlessness and the Power of Prayer.* "A knowledge of my utter strengthlessness and of the power of the Name and the Blood of Jesus in prayer as never before."

- ★ *A Greater Anointing in Witnessing and Preaching.* "An unction in witnessing and preaching greater than ever before."

* *Greater Control of Our Human Tongue.* "A control of the 'unruly member' in daily life since the Lord took peculiar charge of my tongue."

* *Greater Awareness of Spiritual Warfare.* "A clearer understanding of the mighty works of the Holy Spirit and of evil spirits, in these last days of the Present Age."

Supernatural Intercession. William MacArthur found great value in intercession at the throne through praying in tongues, writing of "the blessedness of this experience—the heavenly intoxication of the supernatural song, or the blissful agony of supernatural intercession; yet these are among the blessings indicated in our Apostle's description of the Spirit-filled life—to quote him further, he says: 'Praying with all prayer and supplication in the spirit.'"

I have found great power in interceding for others in tongues. Once I was driving by my church, and the Holy Spirit led me to stop, go inside, kneel at the altar. He brought to my mind a teenage girl and gave me a burden to pray for her for half an hour in tongues. The girl had been set free from demonic bondage, having been involved in a coven of witches. I found out later that at the very time I was praying, the girl had come under intense temptation to return to the occult coven. She was able to overcome the temptation and retain her victory.

Double Equipment of Mind and Spirit. William MacArthur's wife had expressed tongues as the "residue of the anointing." MacArthur himself found it to be even more, considering it to becoming doubly equipped in both mind and spirit: "We do not say that these things cannot be enjoyed in the understanding as well; but Paul had the double equipment, which he so much desired that the others also should enjoy, and declared he would pray and sing with both his spirit and his understanding."

Deeper Death in Surrender to God. Praying in tongues is surrendering our will to God's. Mary Mullen, a respected missionary to

Africa, had no desire to speak in tongues, asking other gifts from God instead. She was convicted about this and surrendered to God:

> I had longed for a deeper death, and an experience where the power of God would be manifested in my life. . . . This desire deepened, and the death deepened. . . . About this time we had a special season of waiting upon the Lord for a deeper revelation of Himself, and one night . . . the joy of the Lord flooded my entire being, until it seemed I could not stay in this world. Then the Spirit seemed to say, 'Now I am ready for the tongue,' and I said, 'Lord I covet the best gifts, please answer my prayer for love, wisdom and power to intercede for others.' This seemed to check the outpouring of the Spirit, and I said, 'Lord, if you want my tongue to speak an unknown language, take it, take it,' and the third 'take it' was spoken in another language, and for a few minutes I talked to Him in a tongue unknown.

This was my own personal experience as well. I did not want to speak in tongues. I prayed, "Lord, give me Your better gifts, not tongues, the least of Your gifts." The Lord spoke to me, just as clear as if it had been audible, "If you are not willing to receive what you consider the least of My gifts, what makes you think you should receive any gifts?" I repented, and replied to the Lord, "Lord, I want what You want. If you want me to speak in tongues, I want to speak in tongues. If you don't want me to speak in tongues, I don't want to speak in tongues." When I surrendered to His will, He graced me with the gift more than forty years ago, and it has been a wonderful source of blessing in my devotional and intercessory prayer life ever since.

Increased Depths of the Spirit. Carrie Judd Montgomery wrote of the greater depths of life in the Spirit that she and her friends experienced through throne utterance: "One lady I had known for years as a sanctified and anointed teacher of God's Word. She was not satisfied and pressed on by faith into the fullness of the Holy Spirit. Her experience was most satisfactory, such appreciation for the blood, such power to witness, increased intercessory prayer, such a baptism of divine love. She spoke in tongues, but kept the gift in its proper place. One of the dear Beulah workers also received the fullness, and we all could realize the increased depths of sweetness, humility, and power which took possession of her life."

Rejuvenation of Body and Mind. Mattie Perry had been an evangelist, pioneering district superintendent, and church planter with the Christian and Missionary Alliance. She had also founded Elhanan Bible Institute and Children's Home. However, she became weak and disabled. When she experienced throne utterance in tongues, she recalled, "The old, tired feeling went like the dropping of an old garment. My memory was quickened and my nerves steadied instantly." She was healed and then ministered with a greater evangelistic and healing ministry. She found throne utterance in tongues to be therapeutic, healing to her body and soul.

Throne Utterances in Your Own Language. Some people may not speak in an unidentified tongue, but they can be so caught up to the throne, that their own native language takes on a heavenly dimension. This was the experience of illiterate schoolboys during the Welsh revival of 1904, when they were transformed by the Spirit of God and their crude language of the street was heightened into perfect high Welsh.

It is not only the illiterate whose speech was transformed, but about 20 years later, Dr. T.J. McCrossan, a Presbyterian Greek scholar, became overwhelmed by the power of the Holy Spirit in a meeting with healing evangelist Charles Price. He fell on the floor in a trance for nearly two hours, raised by the Spirit into the throne room of the heavenlies. McCrossan recalled his experience:

One night the blessed Holy Spirit came down upon me. I saw a light, far brighter than the noon-day sun—a perfect blaze of glory. Hundreds of tongues of fire seemed to dart forth upon and about me. For an hour or more great billows of glory, indescribably beautiful from light and colors, began to roll through my soul like mighty breakers over a sandy beach. No outsider needed to tell me that the Holy Spirit had entered my life in a new way. Then the blessed Spirit took possession of my tongue, and for an hour or more made me praise the Lord Jesus in a way I had never praised Him before. I was literally speaking with another tongue as the Spirit gave to me to utter forth, but it was all in English."

Here was a man well-lettered, but he became so overwhelmed with his visions of the heavenlies, that even his articulate speech was enhanced beyond anything of his own education. He was no longer in control; the Holy Spirit took possession of his tongue. He went on to join Charles Price in healing evangelism ministry, and to become a pastor in the Christian and Missionary Alliance, and a professor at Simpson Bible Institute. One of his young female students learned from his experiences of the Spirit and became close friends with his daughter. That young woman—Kathryn Kuhlman—later launched her own dynamic healing ministry.

Mary Gainforth was pastor of a Christian and Missionary Alliance church in Toronto, Canada, with a healing ministry. She had a similar experience of "tongues of glory" in her own native language:

My whole being was filled with the glory of God. Wave after wave passed over my soul until every thing seemed like a bright shining light. I could see nothing of this world and still I realized what was going on. . . . All I could say was, Glory! Glory!

Some were expecting that I would speak in an unknown tongue. For nine days there was such a halo of glory over me that I could wake up in the night and for hours I could feel the glory of the Lord surging through my mortal frame. God said, 'Are you not satisfied with your tongue of glory?' And I said, 'Yes, Lord.' It just seemed that I could not stand any more of this demonstration of the power of God.

Now when the power of the Spirit comes on me, I have to say, glory, three times before I get my own tongue back again as it was before. No matter what the people may think or say, I know that I have experienced the tongues of glory, what God wanted me to have.

Utterance from the throne may come as tongues of angels—unknown to men, tongues of men—but unknown to the person praying, or tongues of men—speech elevated into the heavenlies, beyond our human capacity. In each case, it is words from the throne of God.

Songs from the Throne

Throne utterances may come as songs from the heavenly places, in which we are lifted up to worship with the heavenly choir. Paul bids us, "Be filled with the Spirit, speaking to one another in psalms and hymns and spiritual songs, singing and making melody with your heart to the Lord" (Eph 5:18b-19). When we are filled with the Spirit, we are stirred to sing from our hearts words from the heart. They are "spiritual songs," songs of the Spirit—spontaneous outbursts in new melodies and words, both known and unknown. This is what we call "singing in the Spirit."

God may give us a melody and words from our own language, or we may go beyond into another language. Charles Wesley expressed this desire in his hymn, "O for a thousand tongues to sing my great Redeemer's praise, the glories of my God and King, the triumphs of His grace." Paul describes this throne utterance of song as "singing with the spirit," bearing witness that this was his own experience as well: "I will sing with the spirit and I will sing with the mind also" (1 Cor 14:15).

Spontaneous New Song. During a nine-week Higher Life revival in Tennessee in 1903, a woman was caught up in the Spirit and spontaneously sang a new song about the Second Coming of Christ. She walked all around the congregation singing, then stopped, lifted her hands to heaven and remained silent and motionless. The congregation "sat spellbound," then one man began shouting praises, and then the whole congregation burst forth in shouting and praises spontaneously. Testimonies "were like artesian wells," people were convicted, saved, and filled with the Spirit.

A Melody from Within the Veil—From Another World. A throne utterance of tongues in song occurred during the 1907 revival in A.B. Simpson's church in New York City. Eyewitnesses reported of the awesome presence of God:

> "A young girl came under the power and her spirit was caught up to the throne. She sang a melody, without words, that seemed to come from within the veil, it was so heavenly. It seemed to come from another world."

> "It seemed as if the very gates of heaven were opened for a little while to the ears of mortals."

Intoxication of Supernatural Song. William MacArthur likened this throne utterance to being drunk in the Spirit, hailing "the blessedness of this experience—the heavenly intoxication of the supernatural song, ... Paul had the double equipment, which he so much desired that the others also should enjoy, and declared he would pray and sing with both his spirit and his understanding."

Drawn into the Presence of God. T.J. McCrossan was enthralled that throne utterance in song lifted people into the manifest Presence of God: "We have frequently heard young people sing in other tongues, as the Spirit gave them utterance; singing with a voice so vastly superior to their own natural voice, that there was no comparison. No interpreter was present on these occasions, and yet I felt certain these were genuine languages (having studied five different languages), and I know from the tone, facial expression and marvelous joy that it was the work of the Holy Spirit. There was something about it so sweet, so attractive, so helpful, something that actually drew one into the very presence of God."[173]

Celestial Harmony from My Innermost Being. Alice Reynolds, a teenage girl in the early Christian and Missionary Alliance, experienced what she called "a heavenly choir": ". . . a low humming that gradually rose in harmonious crescendo as six individuals in different parts of the audience rose spontaneously to their feet and a full tide of glorious melody poured forth in ecstatic worship and praise. . . . from my innermost being heavenly music poured forth like strains through the pipes of some great organ. . . . the flowing forth of celestial harmony like a foretaste of divine rapture."

Singing with a Heavenly Choir. David Wesley Myland, a C&MA pastor and district superintendent was terribly burned from a furnace explosion and had nearly died. He was miraculously healed and burst out speaking and singing in tongues. He saw a vision of Jesus, heaven, and a heavenly choir:

> Presently as they seemed to come to a pause in the singing, at the end of a strain, He turned around so gracefully to me, and looked at me and said, 'Well, My child, what would you like to have?' And I said, 'Oh, Lord, I would like to join Your choir,' and then I seemed to tremble at what I had said, 'join that choir!' He turned and looked toward the choir, and then at me and said, 'My child, you may,' and then all the strength left me, and I said, 'Well, I can't now, I wouldn't dare.' But He made a motion to me with His baton, and it seemed I was lifted right up and was set down in the choir.
>
> I began to sing with them a little and what do you suppose? I was singing the 'latter rain' song in tongues, which I afterwards interpreted and wrote into English. They all seemed to join in with me and after it was all over they sang another great chorus. I listened, and the great Leader, my glorified Christ, motioned to me and I sat down, and I thought, Oh, what singing! The old Ohio Quartette never could sing like that and I found myself singing also. . . .

Oh, what glory I was in for an hour. I took out my watch and saw that for just an hour I was lost to this world. Oh, what a vision of Jesus and of heaven! Indescribable! I have just sketched the outline. Oh, what glory there was in my soul.

A Perfect Song—Transcendently Beyond This World. A.B. Simpson's music leader Henry Kenning describes hearing a similar heavenly experience: "Something in the tone of voice gripped my soul. . . . I listened to the song [in tongues], and I seemed entranced. . . . I was dumbfounded. Such purity of tone, such perfect poise of resonance, such evenness of the registers ascending and descending, and most remarkable of all, such astounding breath-control as I have never heard. . . . too beautiful for words . . . indeed eloquent with a message from another world. . . . with all the beauty and rapture that the voice seemed to speak, there was an indefinable and indescribable *something* that seemed to breathe the holiest and profoundest worship. . . . merged in something transcendently beyond—the worship and adoration of God."

Vibrant with Rapturous Response—Satiated with God Himself. Henry Kenning received his own Pentecost, testifying:

There came over me a sense of God's overshadowing presence, and I felt there was nothing to do but to bend lower and lower under the weight of His overshadowing. . . . by the blessed constraint of the Spirit, I was prostrated at His feet. . . . from the very inner springs of my being there began to well up a wordless melody of praise and thanksgiving to God. After a little while, without any conscious effort of my mind or will, there flowed sweetly and calmly utterances in another tongue in perfect cadence and rhythm. My whole being was vibrant with rapturous response. . . I was satisfied, satisfied, satisfied, not with the new song in a new tongue, not with the ecstacy [sic], but with God, with Himself.

You Too Can Experience Throne Utterance!

As you seek God and His presence at His throne, you will sometimes fail for words in the presence of an awesome God. At some point you may feel you need to burst out in prayer or praise in expressions beyond what you can say. May your prayer be that of Charles Wesley:

> O for a thousand tongues to sing
> My great Redeemer's praise
> The glories of my God and King
> The triumphs of His grace!

For Reflection

1. Have you ever experienced praying and singing in tongues, or known someone who has? What was the experience like? Does it compare with these experiences?

2. What questions do you have about praying and singing in tongues?

CHAPTER 13

Throne Faith—
The Faith of God

"Let us draw near . . . in full assurance of faith" (Heb 10:22).

"Have the faith of God" (Mark 11:22, literal translation).

J esus calls us to come up higher in faith! He bids us to have throne faith—the faith of God Himself, the fullness of faith, the faith that has no doubt and gets our prayers answered.

Many types or levels of faith can be identified in Scripture. The highest level of faith is what classic writers called "throne faith" or the "faith of God"—the faith that comes from the very throne of God and is the faith of God Himself. In fact, although many translate Mark 11:22 as "Have faith in God," when you look at the original language, Jesus literally declared, "Have the faith *of* God."

Jesus is bidding us to have the faith of God Himself, the faith that comes from the very throne of God. Throne faith is the faith that is a perfect, full, complete faith, lacking nothing.

Can God Have Faith?

"But wait a minute," someone may understandably ask, "Can God have faith?" If you mean, "Can God have faith in the sense of putting trust in and reliance upon a human being or a force?," certainly not. God as all-knowing, all-powerful, and everywhere-present, is far above and beyond that. Certainly, if the nature of faith is understood solely as a human quality of passive trust in someone human or something else, then obviously God cannot have faith.

However, as Andrew Murray explains in *Holiest of All*, "Faith as an active power. . . . is thus much more than trust in the word of another. . . ." Murray recognized that with the elliptical nature of truth, there is a pole of active faith as well as passive trust. As A.W. Tozer puts it, "Truth has two wings." Faith has two wings—passive trust in another and active faith that is exercised.

Faith as an Active Force of God's Nature. If we understand faith as a force or energy or power as a divine attribute emanating out of the very nature of God's omnipotence (as taught by many leaders throughout church history like Clement of Alexandria, Charles Spurgeon, and A.B. Simpson), then, yes, God can exercise faith. A.B. Simpson explains, "Indeed it seems faith is the principle upon which God Himself acts, the secret of His power in creating matter and in commanding the events of providence. . . .The faith of God must mean the faith that God Himself exercises." [174] It is a part of His all-powerful divine nature. This does not limit God in any way.

Faith as Mutual Trust Between God as Father, Son, and Holy Spirit. The members of the Trinity have faith in one another—God the Father has faith in the Son and the Spirit. Jesus the Son has faith in the Father and the Spirit. The Spirit has faith in the Father and the Son. The Trinity has a mutual dependence upon one another.

As God, He has absolute confidence, absolute faith, perfect faith in Himself, the other members of the Godhead, and in the fulfillment of His will. He doubts nothing. He walks fully by faith, not by human sight. He sees the past, present, and future. He sees the unseen, the invisible. He acts in full assurance.

So for us as believers to exercise the faith of God, it means that our faith arises to the level of God's confidence in Himself, the Trinity, and the fulfillment of His will. It is the "God-kind of faith." It is the faith of the throne, faith from the throne.

Understanding Throne Faith[175]

Throne Faith Is Not Elementary Faith. Paul declared. "The life I live now in the flesh, I live by the faith of the Son of God, who loved me and gave His life for me" (Gal 2:20). Oswald Chambers recognized that Paul did not mean "faith *in* Jesus," but rather he comments that the "faith of the Son of God" is "not elementary faith in Jesus," but rather "the faith which is in the Son of God," "the very faith which governed Jesus Christ."[176] It is the faith that Jesus Himself exercised as the Son of God, not an elementary level of faith, but a complete, perfect faith. It is that faith that we now can live by as well.

Throne Faith Is Not Our Faith. A.B. Simpson counseled, "Faith is hindered most of all by what we call 'our faith,'" advising, "Jesus does not say to us, 'Have great faith yourselves.' But He does say, 'have the faith of God.'" Charles Spurgeon cautioned, "Faith must not be above the divine source of all blessing that lies in the grace of God. Never make a Christ of your faith. . . . Our life is found in looking unto Jesus (Heb 12:2), not in looking to our own faith. By faith all things become possible to us, yet the power is not in the faith but in the God upon whom faith relies."[177]

Throne Faith Is God's Measure of Faith. Carrie Judd Montgomery encourages us that "Jesus is the author and finisher of our faith, and He will work *His own faith* in our hearts. Let us give up our own poor attempts at faith and take the faith of the Son of

God. The Lord Jesus has faith in His own power to make good all His promises."[178]

Smith Wigglesworth understood that our own faith is inadequate: "Oh, this wonderful faith of the Lord Jesus. Your faith comes to an end. How many times I have been to the place where I have had to tell the Lord, 'I have used all the faith I have,' and then He has placed His own faith within me." Wigglesworth counseled, "We have got to get rid of our small measure of faith, because God's measure is so much greater than ours."[179]

Throne Faith Is Mountain-Moving Faith. Classic faith leaders recognized that this faith in Mark 11:22-24 is a "mountain-moving faith," that is, a gift of faith from God, not the ordinary everyday exercise of faith. This type of faith is given by God only on special occasions. Fourth-century church father Cyril of Jerusalem identified this mountain-moving faith of which Jesus speaks with the gift of faith in 1 Cor 12:9, designating it as "bestowed by Christ as a gift of grace." Chrysostom calls this kind of faith "the mother of miracles." This is the faith that does not doubt (Mark 11:22-24; James 1:6-7), which A.B. Simpson calls "a special work of the Holy Ghost."

Throne Faith Is Implicit Trust without Doubt. Healing evangelist Charles Price exhorts us, "Get some of God's faith. . . . You simply cannot believe without the alloy of doubt until you have the faith of God. It takes God's faith to clean up these human hearts of ours of all the debris, the fears, misgivings and doubts."[180] E.M. Bounds identified such mountain-moving faith as implicit trust: "When a Christian believer attains to faith of such magnificent proportions as these, he steps into the realm of implicit trust. He stands without a tremor on the apex of his spiritual outreaching."[181] Oral Roberts expressed this as such a confidence in God that "you know that you know that you know that you know."

Throne Faith Is Imparted, Not Worked Up. Chambers asserted that Paul's faith was not in his faith in Christ, "but the faith that the Son of God has imparted to him."[182] Greek professor T.J. McCrossan taught: "This 'faith of God' is the faith the Holy Ghost imparts to God's saints, just in proportion as we allow Him to control our lives. 1 Corinthians 12:9 tells us that 'faith' is one of the gifts of the Spirit, and this 'Spirit-imparted faith' is the faith of God."[183] Referring to putting on the armor of God, Spurgeon counseled, "Your faith must be of heaven's forging, or your shield will certainly fail you."[184]

Throne Faith Is Supernatural Faith. Biblical commentators have historically understood the "faith of God" expressed in Mark 11:22-24 as the very highest kind of faith, a "'supernatural' degree of faith." Adam Clarke viewed it as "the strongest faith." Greek scholar A.T. Robertson defined it as "the God kind of faith." Andrew Murray called "fullness of faith" as "supernatural, above what you can think."[185]

Throne Faith Is the Zenith of Faith. Mountain-moving faith is the very faith of God, or perfect faith, the ultimate or zenith of faith. Watchman Nee commented on Mark 11:22-24, "Only with perfect faith may one speak to the mountain."[186] E.M. Bounds identified such mountain-moving faith in God, not as ordinary, everyday faith, but as the summit of a peak: "When a Christian believer attains to faith of such magnificent proportions as these, he steps into the realm of implicit trust. He stands without a tremor on the apex of his spiritual outreaching. He has attained faith's veritable topstone which is unswerving, unalterable, unalienable trust in the power of the living God."[187]

Throne Faith Enters into the Holy of Holies. *Faith* enters within the veil!," Puritan Thomas Brooks declares. Andrew Murray understood that "fullness of faith" to enter into the Holy of Holies is "supernatural, above what you can think." When we have the very fullest of faith, a faith that does not doubt, we enter in to the Holiest of All, the very Shekinah Glory of God.

Throne Faith Is Authoritative Faith. Such faith, then, is the highest measure of faith and has the highest operational authority of any kind of faith. A.T. Pierson taught "the authority of faith," that is, the authority to command in faith. When our faith rises to this level, we can exercise what early holiness writer George Peck called, "throne language," that is, the prayer of faith and the command of faith.

Practically Applying Throne Faith

Throne faith, then, is not our doing, but God's. We are lifted to the throne. We don't work up our faith, we don't struggle to pull our faith up. Faith is imparted to us. His faith lifts us up. We are lifted up to throne faith by the following practices:

Have Confidence in Christ. Puritan Thomas Brooks envisioned this glorious truth: "By an eye of faith, through the telescope of a promise—we look into heaven. The *people* of Israel stood in the outer court of the temple—but the *high-priest* 'entered within the veil,' into the holy of holies; thus the *senses* stand in the outward court of the body—but *faith* enters within the veil! It sees Christ clothed with the robe of our human nature, and sitting down in glory above the angels. Faith embraces Christ. . . . how shall I put out a long arm to reach Christ in heaven? 'Believe,' says he, 'and you have laid hold on him!' Faith is the *golden clasp* that joins us to Christ."

Claim and Confess Our Faith. A.B. Simpson exhorted, "We must claim the faith of God, letting the Spirit of Jesus sustain our faith with His strong faith."[188] This is not naming and claiming anything we want, but naming and claiming anything God wants. Oswald Chambers wrote of the importance of confessing our faith according to Romans 10:9-10 in order to lift us into the heavenly realms: "In the Bible confession and testimony are put in a prominent place, and the test of a person's moral character is his 'say so.' I may try and make myself believe a hundred and one things, but it will never be mine until I 'say so.' If I say with myself what I believe and confess it with my mouth, I am lifted into the domain of that thing."[189]

Recognize God as the Source or Author of Faith. Spurgeon preached: "It is literally, 'Have the faith of God'—the faith which is wrought in us by God, and sustained by God, for that is the only faith that is worth the living. . . . He is the author, the giver, and the nourisher of faith."[190]

Rely upon the Faithfulness of God. J. Hudson Taylor understood the "faith of God" as the faithfulness of God, God's covenant loyalty. He interpreted Mark 11:22 as "Reckon on God's faithfulness," commenting, "I could not reckon on my faith but I could reckon on God's faithfulness."[191] Andrew Murray cited Hebrews 11:11, "By faith Sarah . . . counted him [God] faithful who had promised," commenting, "The faithfulness of God was . . . her faith."

Live by the Faith of Jesus Christ Himself. "The life which I now live in the flesh I live by the faith of the Son of God. . ." (Gal 2:20, KJV). Oswald Chambers explains, "Literally, the faith that was in Christ Jesus is now in me."[192] Watchman Nee likewise commented on this Scripture, "When we believe and receive the Son of God, not only His life but His faith, too, enters into us. Hence we may live by *His* faith."[193]

Take Hold of God's Own Faith. Paul confessed, "I press on so that I may lay hold of that for which also I was laid hold of by Christ Jesus" (Phil 3:12). We don't passively receive faith; we grasp it for ourselves. F.F. Bosworth wrote about "the faith that takes." Likewise, A.W. Tozer quoted Meister Eckhart: "God's gifts are meted out according to the taker, not according to the giver." It is the God-kind of faith that can take hold and believe without doubting. After exhorting to "Have the faith of God," Jesus explains, "Therefore I say to you, all things for which you pray and ask, believe that you have received them, and they will be granted you" (Mark 11:24).

The Greek word for "receive" here is the *lambano*, which implies a more active taking, as opposed to *dechomai*, which implies a more passive acceptance. Literally then, Jesus is saying "Believe that you take hold of them and they shall be granted you." As Andrew Murray observes: "All spiritual blessings must be received, that is, accepted or taken in faith. . . . The Greek word for receiving and taking is the same. . . . Receiving not only implies God's bestowment, but our acceptance."[194] The faith of God is an active exercise of faith as the very power of God. Faith is not trust or hope in some unknown future, but confidently seeing the unseen.

Ask for Special Faith. Some people try to work up or exercise their faith by abandoning medical treatment. A.B. Simpson, however, cautioned, "If you have any question about your faith for this, make it a special matter of preparation and prayer. Ask God to give you special faith for this act. All our graces must come from Him, and faith among the rest. We have nothing of our own, and even our very faith is but the grace of Christ Himself within us. We can exercise it, and thus far our responsibility extends; but He must impart it, and we simply put it on and wear it as from Him."[195] This is "Spirit-imparted" faith, as classic devotional writer Mrs. Charles Cowman explains, "The faith of God is in-wrought within our hearts by the Holy Ghost."[196] Pray for the Holy Spirit to impart such faith to you.

Feed Constantly on the Word of God. Wigglesworth distinguished between natural faith, and supernatural faith that is a gift from God. He recognized that hearing from God is needed to exercise this special faith, which is the faith of God:

> All lack of faith is due to not feeding on God's Word. . . . Feed on the living Christ of whom this Word is full. As you get taken up with the glorious fact and the wondrous presence of the living Christ, the faith of God will spring up within you. "Faith cometh by hearing and hearing by the word of Christ.". . . . Seek God until you get from Him a mighty revelation of the Son, until that inward revelation moves you on to the place where you are always steadfast, unmovable, and always abounding in the work of the Lord.[197]

Develop a Supernaturally Natural Faith. While this is a special, supernatural faith, some faith leaders recognized that such faith, through exercise, could become what we might today call "supernaturally natural." Carrie Judd Montgomery commented of this commanding, mountain-moving faith of Mark 11:22-24, "God wants us all to have this faith. He desires to bring His children up to an every-day, working faith for all the difficulties that arise." This faith is not developing the God-kind of faith that we already have, but God imparting to us more faith as we use the faith we have. Similarly, George Müller encouraged people that as we exercise the faith we have, more faith is given. The every-day measure of faith develops into a supernatural gift of faith.

Exercise the Prayer of Faith. R.A. Torrey taught that the prayer of faith of Mark 11:22-24 is "prayer that the Holy Spirit inspires." This is not prayer from our own minds, but Spirit-inspired faith prayer. James declared that "the prayer of faith shall heal the sick" (James 5:15). Torrey explains, "It is not always possible to pray 'the prayer of faith,' only when God makes it possible by the leading of the Holy Spirit." [198] If we are in tune with the Spirit and praying out of our position on God's throne, then we can pray with confidence that our prayer is being answered.

Exercise Authoritative Faith to Speak to the Mountain. MacMillan understood the exercise of spiritual authority to be not merely prayer. Rather, prayer paves the way for the exercise of authority, but does not substitute for it. The exercise of authority, then, involves "command of faith" based on Jesus' statement in Mark 11:22-24, exhorting disciples to speak to the mountain: "The question involved is not that of an imposing faith, but that of an all-sufficient Name. . . . As he speaks to the mountain in the name of Christ, he puts his hand on the dynamic force that controls the universe. Heavenly energy is released, and his behest is obeyed." [199]

Believers are not merely to pray to God about our problems, but to speak an authoritative word in the name of Jesus directed to the problems. A.B. Simpson advocates this assertiveness of faith in prayer: "In the name of Jesus we are to not only ask, but claim and pass in the orders of faith to the bank of heaven."[200] Expounding on Mark 11:22-24, Higher Life teacher A.T. Pierson comments:

> The coincidence is too remarkable to be either accidental or unimportant. In all these cases it is not "pray" but "say," not the word of petition but of direction, not as a suppliant but as of a sovereign. This we regard as the central, vital heart of this great lesson on Faith. The Master of all girds the servant with His own power and entrusts him with authority to command. Faith claims not only blessing but power to bless.[201]

Know When to Command in Faith. One of the most controversial and misunderstood concepts of Throne Faith is the idea of commanding faith, based on Isaiah 45:11, in which God says, "Ask of Me of things to come concerning my sons, and concerning the work of my hands command ye me" (KJV). E.M. Bounds claims this verse is "God's *carte blanche* to prayer."[202] MacMillan explained this controversy:

> So unreasonable to the natural mind seems the proposition of Jehovah to His people (Isa 45:11) that they should "command" Him concerning the work of His hands, that various alternative readings of the passage have been made with the intent of toning down the apparent extravagance of the divine offer. Men are slow to believe that the Almighty really means exactly what He says. They think it a thing incredible that He would share with human hands the throttle of divine power. Nor have they the spiritual understanding to comprehend the purpose of the Father to bring those who have been redeemed with the precious blood of His dear Son into living and practical cooperation with that Son in the administration of His kingdom.[203]

Let us be clear that this does not mean that we control God. This does not mean that you can name and claim anything you want. Rather, this is the kind of faith Spurgeon speaks of—you are a decree of God. Spurgeon declared: "Thou art thyself a decree. . . . Our prayers are God's decrees in another shape. . . ."[204] This does not mean that you can go around decreeing anything you want. So when can we appropriately command in faith? When can we decree?

- **We Can Command in Faith When We Are in Harmony with God.** A.T. Pierson commented on this Scripture as well, asserting: "Faith in God so unites to God that it passes beyond the privilege of asking to the power of commanding. . . . And so—marvelous fact! The child of God, laying hold by faith of the Power of the Omnipotent One, issues his fiat. . . ."[205]

- **We Can Command in Faith When We Are Obedient to God's Laws.** Pierson declares, "Obey the Law of the Power and the Power obeys you. Conform to the Laws and modes of the Spirit's operations, and in the work of God's hands you may command the Spirit's Power."[206] Obedience to God is power-ful—power-filled. It puts power in our hands and our voices. We can declare, "Come Your Kingdom, be done Your will, on earth as it is in heaven."

- **We Can Command in Faith When We Are Led by the Holy Spirit in the Will of God.** Spurgeon explains:

  > Do not say, "How can my prayers affect the decrees?" They cannot, except in so much as your prayers are decrees, and that as they come out, every prayer that is inspired of the Holy Ghost unto your soul is as omnipotent and eternal as that decree which said, "Let there be light and there was light." . . . The ear of God Himself shall listen, and the hand of God Himself shall yield to thy will. God bids thee cry, "Thy will be done," and thy will shall be done. When thou canst plead His promise, then thy will is His will.[207]

You can only decree what God reveals to you that He wants. You can only name and claim what God reveals to you that He wants.

- *We Can Command in Faith Only Reverently and Humbly, Not Brazenly.* Pierson writes of the power of commanding, "This lesson is at first sight so astounding as to seem incredible—it passes all understanding, and faith itself staggers at such promises. Let us reverently seek to take in the marvelous thought."[208] Only when our motives are right before God can we exercise such authority.

Put Your Hand on the Throne

When your hand touches the throne of God, faith from the throne is imparted to you and through you. God desires to transform your faith into His faith. Paul declared, "The righteousness of God is revealed from faith to faith" (Rom 1:17), literally "out of faith into faith"—out of one sphere of faith into another, a higher sphere of faith. He desires to raise you from a lower degree of faith to a higher degree of faith—indeed, even the highest. Whenever we touch heaven, we can pray with a perfect confidence that our prayer will be answered. When we hear from the throne, we can even command in faith, because the commands come from the throne, not ourselves. Take hold of the throne today!

For Reflection

1. In what ways have you experienced throne faith?

2. How can you experience throne faith more fully in your own life?

CHAPTER 14

Throne Provision & Prosperity

"Beloved, I pray that in all respects you may prosper and be in good health, just as your soul prospers" (3 John 2).

"Give, and it will be given unto you. They will pour into your lap a good measure—pressed down, shaken together, and running over. For by your standard of measure it will be measured to you in return" (Luke 6:38).

Live Long and Prosper!

For Star Trek fans (and you know from the first chapter that I am one of them), one of our classic mottos is Spock's greeting, "Live long and prosper." This has also been the mantra (sometimes for better and sometimes for worse) of the so-called "Prosperity Gospel." Nevertheless, excesses aside, Throne Life does include a biblical concept of "Throne Prosperity." God does want us to live long and prosper.

Puritan leader Thomas Brooks and Baptist Charles Spurgeon taught that the blessings of Deuteronomy 28 are for the Christian in covenant relationship with God now in this life. Renowned Philadelphia Baptist pastor Russell Conwell, who founded Temple University and Conwell School of Theology, preached his famous prosperity message "Acres of Diamonds" 6,000 times throughout the United States, citing from Scripture that "hard work and godly living would and should result in wealth." In fact, he believed that becoming wealthy in order to use that wealth wisely was a Christian's responsibility.

The Baptists had a prosperity gospel; the Puritans had a prosperity gospel; the holiness movements had a prosperity gospel—but they were balanced. The Puritan prosperity gospel was balanced with hard work and godly living; the Baptist prosperity gospel was balanced with generous giving; the holiness prosperity gospel was balanced with death to self. A true biblical prosperity gospel is not self-centered, but focused on how we can bless others.

Throne Prosperity Means, First of All and Primarily, Prosperity of Soul. A.B. Simpson and other Higher Life leaders of his day understood 3 John 2 as a prayer inspired by God, asserting, "We may expect to be 'in health' and prosper 'even as our soul prospers.'" This means that health and material prosperity are interrelated with the spiritual and emotional state of the soul: "It implies that we cannot expect the Lord's blessing upon our bodies and our business, if we cherish in our hearts those spiritual conditions which bring divine chastening and produce misery and pain."[209] If our soul is not prospering, that is, if we have impure motives or we lack God's peace and contentment in our circumstances, we will not experience prosperity in our physical and financial lives. God does want His people to prosper materially, so long as that is not our focus. Simpson assures us, "There is no harm whatever in having money, houses, lands, friends and dearest children if you do not value these things for themselves."[210]

Throne Prosperity Represents the Father's Care. Hannah Whitall Smith likened the life of faith to the relationship of a child in the heavenly Father's house. Giving the example of an adopted child she visited in a wealthy home, she explained, "If nothing would so grieve and wound the loving hearts around her as to see this little child beginning to be worried or anxious about herself in any way,—about whether her food and clothes would be provided, or how she was to get her education or her future support,—how much more must the great, loving heart of our God and Father be grieved and wounded at seeing His children taking so much anxious care and thought! . . . Who is the best cared for in every household? Is it not the little children?"[211]

Throne Prosperity Means Provision for All Needs and God's Work. Prosperity, biblically, is not primarily wealth or getting one's desires, but supply for all of our needs and accomplishing God's work. Higher Life leaders like Charles Cullis, Hudson Taylor, Charles Spurgeon, Amy Carmichael, and A.B. Simpson practiced living by faith in similar manner as that of George Müller, trusting God daily for financial and physical provision for their ministries.

Hannah Whitall Smith understood that "Better and sweeter than health, or friends, or money, or fame, or prosperity, is the adorable will of God."[212] This is not to say that God does not care about our material welfare, because God *is* interested in providing for our needs. Rather, the focus is not in getting, but trusting.

Throne Prosperity Transforms the Earthly to the Heavenly. A.W. Tozer writes of the transmutation of wealth in the kingdom of God, which he calls the highest wealth: "One of the glories of the Christian religion is that faith and love can transmute lower values into higher ones. Earthly possessions can be turned into heavenly treasures. . . . As base a thing as money often is, it yet can be transmuted into everlasting treasure. It can be converted into food for the hungry and clothing for the poor; it can keep a missionary actively winning lost men to the light of the gospel and thus transmute itself into heavenly values. Any temporal possession can be turned into everlasting wealth. Whatever is given to Christ is immediately touched with immortality."[213]

Throne Prosperity Means Throne Abundance. Lack of anything needed for the kingdom of God is non-existent at the throne of God. In fact, everything needed for kingdom living is found in abundance. Jesus assures us, "I came that they may have life, and have it abundantly" (John 10:10). Throne Life in the heavenly places is an abundant life. Ruth Paxson explains: "The spiritual man has enough and to spare. He does not have to hoard his spiritual riches for he is the child of a King and knows that his Father is a royal Giver and has taught His child 'that it is more blessed to give than to receive.' He is assured that the more he gives the more he will receive. Out of his innermost being flow the rivers of living water to bring life more abundant to every life he touches. . . A life lived on the highest plane is a continuous miracle of God's grace."

Throne Prosperity Demonstrates Contentment in All Circumstances. Throne Life understands that we can enjoy the prosperity of God regardless of our circumstances. A.B. Simpson cited fourteenth century German mystic John Tauler, "I have never been unprosperous, for I know how to live with God." If we are living in the presence of the heavenly throne, then no matter what our earthly situation, we can with confidence declare that we are prospering. Hudson Taylor, who experienced severe privations as a missionary, nevertheless had a similar attitude looking back over his years of ministry, amazingly saying, "I never made a sacrifice."

What an attitude! Never made a sacrifice? You can only maintain that confidence if you are abiding with Christ in the heavenlies.

These people of faith had learned with the Apostle Paul: "I have learned to be content in whatever circumstances I am. I know how to get along with humble means, and I also know how to live in prosperity; in any and every circumstance I have learned the secret of being filled and going hungry, both of having abundance and suffering need. I can do all things through Him who strengthens me" (Phil 4:11-13).

Throne Prosperity Acts with a Giving Spirit. Taylor's viewpoint on personal prosperity was, "Having now the twofold object in view . . . of accustoming myself to endure hardness, and of economizing in order to help those among whom I was laboring in the Gospel, I soon found that I could live upon very much less than I had previously thought possible. . . . My experience was that the less I spent on myself and the more I gave to others, the fuller of happiness and blessing did my soul become."[214] The attitude or motive for wanting to prosper is a vital key, according to Müller:

> Suppose such a person had heard the promises about prayer, and should say, "Now I will try if these things are true, and I will ask God to give me a hundred thousand pounds sterling, and then I can give myself easy days; I can travel about and enjoy myself." Suppose he prays every day for this large sum of money, will he obtain it? Assuredly not! Why not? He does not ask for it that he may help the poor abundantly; that he may contribute to the work of God more liberally, but he asks that he may spend his life in idleness, and in enjoying the pleasures of the world.[215]

Throne Prosperity Does Not Claim Entitlement. Some people claim that because they are "King's Kids," they deserve first class everything. However, although classic Higher Life leaders recognized their throne rights and privileges, they did not feel always entitled to the best and most expensive of everything. For instance, when Oswald Chambers travelled by ship, he chose neither first class, nor third class, but took the moderate place. On his voyage by ship to America his second class cabin was described as "not luxurious, but much more comfortable than the crowded compartments below."

But is it always wrong to go first class and desire the best? Amy Carmichael usually travelled third class, but on one occasion she traveled first class on a ship in order to get sufficient sleep, cleanliness, privacy, and quiet when recovering from an illness. There were also times when she was willing to "go first class" in her buildings.

She determined that it would be right to spend the Lord's money on more expensive materials if the money was given specifically for that purpose.

A fellow minister told Spurgeon that he was going to take third class on the train "to save the Lord's money." Spurgeon replied, "Well, I am going to the first class section of the train to save the Lord's servant." Spurgeon recognized his legitimate need for better accommodations for his health and rest. So while normally Higher Life leaders would not choose to go first class, they sometimes thought it was appropriate for their well-being. They would spend money for the very best if it was for the good of the Lord's work or for others, not merely for their own convenience and comfort.

I have seen this Throne Life attitude from a United States Senator who I knew to be a Christian. On an airplane flight, I once had an opportunity to meet him and his family, seated just across the aisle behind me. I was surprised and impressed that he was traveling coach, instead of first class, which he could well afford to do. He was a man of graciousness and humility who did not take advantage of his status, exemplifying a true attitude of throne prosperity.

Throne Prosperity Gives Up in Order to Gain. A common classic faith principle taught that abandonment of self is key to gaining the blessings of God. Andrew Murray, for example, asserted that without self-denial and letting go of the world, faith cannot be exercised. Higher Life leaders all taught the biblical principle that abandonment precedes faith. Hannah Whitall Smith called this a "secret" to the Christian's happy or victorious life.

Throne Prosperity Submits to the Will of the Senior Partner. A.B. Simpson advised that Jesus is "not a wealthy friend, advancing a large sum to aid us in our business, but coming into it Himself, and giving us His partnership, His counsel and His whole capital. And it is received by faith. . . . In one single act we renounce ourselves and all our sin and self-confidence, and take Him and His all-sufficiency for every future need."[216] We partner with the very throne of God; what better partnership could we ask for?

Simpson notes that the life of faith requires the continual exercise of a strong will, and "that faith itself is largely the exercise of a sanctified and intensified will, but in order to do this, it is necessary that our will be wholly renounced and God's will invariably accepted instead, and then we can put into it all the strength and force of our being, and will it even as God wills it, because He wills it."[217]

Throne Prosperity Willingly Waives Our Rights. Faith can only be properly exercised by renouncing self and putting on Christ day by day. To those who would claim that prosperity is the covenant right of the believer, Chambers would agree in principle, but answer, "But if you are living the life of faith you will exercise your right to waive your rights, and let God choose for you."[218] Simpson, also emphasized, "The very test of consecration is our willingness . . . to surrender our rights."[219]

Simpson exemplified this attitude regarding material promises, avowing that Christ Himself is the believer's supreme inheritance. He illustrated the point from the Old Testament incident of Abraham and Lot: "He [Abraham] allowed Lot to have his choice of the land, and when he, full of his strong self-life, claimed the best, Abraham let him have it. When we believe God, we can let people have many things which really belong to us. If God has them for us, no one can possibly take them from us. So Lot took the rich plain of the Jordan. God had given it all to Abraham, and he knew he could not lose it."[220] Simpson perceived that it is a matter of motivation and inner attitude.

Throne Prosperity Demonstrates Heavenly Desires. The question involves setting one's affections on heaven rather than on earth. Simpson declared, "Faith [is] yielding up the world because it has a better inheritance." Like Lot, Simpson perceived that people with an "earthly spirit" tend to "contend for the best of the land." However, in contrast, "the man of faith can let the present world go because he knows he has a better world, but even as he lets it go God tells him that all things are his because he is Christ's."[221] Amy Carmichael explains further:

> Those of us who are God's emissaries are to treat the world (not just its corruptions, but its legitimate joys, its privileges and blessings also), as a thing to be touched at a distance. . . . It is not that He forbids us this or that indulgence or comfort. . . . No, it is that we who love our Lord, and we whose affections are set on the things that are heaven for us today—we voluntarily and gladly lay aside things that charm the world, so that we may be charmed and ravished by the things of heaven. . . . to look upon the world, in all its delights and attractions, suspecting that traps are set there for us, reserving ourselves for a higher way. *The world is not for us.*[222]

Throne Prosperity Seeks the Kingdom of God, Not Prosperity. Seeking after prosperity, in the minds of these Higher Life leaders, is contrary to a heavenly-minded mindset. To the spiritually-minded or kingdom-minded, material considerations are secondary. Jesus Himself commanded, "But seek first His kingdom and His righteousness, and all these things will be added unto you" (Matt 6:33). Based on Jesus' words, Oswald Chambers advised, "We are not to seek success or prosperity."[223] If we are seeking the kingdom, we don't need to seek prosperity. If we are seeking God's kingdom with right motives (righteousness), then everything we need *will* be abundantly supplied.

Our attitude determines our altitude. Andrew Murray asserted that seeking after pleasure, honor, and riches actually stifles faith, and "only an unworldly spirit . . . can be strong in faith." An "unworldly spirit" is a heavenly attitude, a throne attitude.

A.B. Simpson taught that the deeper and higher Christian life is not about receiving blessings, but about a change in priorities: "Once it was the blessing, now it is the Lord . . ." Material blessings, although part of the inheritance of the Higher Life, are secondary. An old gospel song expresses this attitude, "My goal is God Himself, not joy, not peace, not even blessing . . ." This is in stark contrast to people who seek God for what they can get from God, not for God Himself.

Dangers Regarding Throne Prosperity

Seeking Your Own Desires as If They Were God's. While classic Higher Life leaders were not opposed to having wealth, they cautioned about the dangers that prosperity can bring. Johann Blumhardt "detested the sort of prayer that presses God for one's own desires."[224] In contrast to the teaching that "you can have what-ever you desire," Smith Wigglesworth commented, "Desire toward God, and you will have desires from God and He will meet you on the line of those desires when you reach out in simple faith."[225]

Amy Carmichael also makes this important differentiation: "God has something much better for us than the thing we naturally desire. As we wait with all the desire of our mind fixed on Him, the thing we naturally long for becomes less pressing, the friction ceases, and we are set free to go on."[226] If we are claiming prosperity for our own pleasure because we are King's Kids, we are not in the will of God, but if we are praying that we may prosper for the sake of others, that prayer reflects God's will.

Equating Material Prosperity with God's Approval. Some people mistakenly associate all financial abundance with God's bless-ing and approval. On the contrary, E.M. Bounds advised, "Material prosperity is not the infallible sign of spiritual prosperity."[227] Rather, prosperity may cause a person to grow farther away from God. Dwight Moody admonished, "We can stand affliction better than we can prosperity, for in prosperity we forget God." Hudson Taylor like-wise cautioned, "While the sun of prosperity shines upon me I may safely enjoy myself here without Him."[228]

Lack of Wisdom and Maturity to Handle Prosperity. A.B. Simpson spoke of the "discipline of prosperity," that working of God in the believer's heart to be able to handle prosperity with a godly attitude:

> How few Christians really know how to abound. How frequently prosperity changes their temper and the habits and fruits of their lives! To receive God's blessing in temporal things, to have wealth suddenly thrust upon us, to be surrounded with the congenial friends, to be enriched with all the happiness that love, home, the world's applause, and unbounded prosperity can give, and yet to keep a humble heart, to be separated from the world in its spirit and in its pleasures, to keep our hearts in holy indifference from the love and need of earthly things, to stand for God as holy witnesses in the most public station, and to use our prosperity and wealth as a sacred trust for Him, counting nothing our own, and still depending upon Him as simply as in the days of penury—this, indeed, is an experience rarely found, and only possible through the infinite grace of God.[229]

Prosperity Can Be Dangerous to Our Spiritual and Physical Health. With his great wit and humor, Spurgeon adds a disclaimer to his own teaching on prosperity, which contemporary prosperity seekers would do good to heed: "Of course, I may not be sure of growing rich. I shall be fat, but not too fat. Too great riches might make me as unwieldy as corpulent persons usually are, and cause me the dyspepsia of worldliness, and perhaps bring on a fatty degeneration of the heart."[230]

Similarly, Carrie Judd Montgomery observes that preoccupation with worldly things can even prevent healing: "If the things of the world are precious to us we will be occupied with them, and will not render unto the Lord according to all that He hath done for us. After a failure of this kind I have often seen it very difficult for people to receive healing again from the hand of the Lord."

Sound Principles of Throne Prosperity

Keeping in mind the dynamic tension that, on one hand, God wants Christians to prosper, and, on the other hand, that our motives must be pure, we will look at some of the classic Throne Life principles for prospering.

Have a Generous, Giving Attitude. Classic Higher Life leaders usually did not legalistically demand a tithe, but they viewed it as a beginning principle of liberality. George Müller viewed tithing, not as a law, but as the minimum basis of generosity. Carrie Judd Montgomery commented that the tithe needs to be sown in faith for the windows of blessing to be opened, claiming "I have many times found by experience that money which has been tithed, lasted much longer than that which had not been tithed."

Oral Roberts' saying, "The tithe is not a debt you owe, but a seed you sow," has its origin in this classic faith understanding of giving, based on Luke 6:38. "Seed faith" is not an invention of the contemporary prosperity movement. Andrew Murray, for instance, refers to exercising faith as a "seed-word." Watchman Nee asserted that the way of God is not to save and get rich, but give and it shall be given.

Oral Roberts has another popular saying derived from this Scripture, "Give to get to give." However, again he is not the originator of the concept, for Spurgeon asserted, almost exactly as Roberts, "Faith's way of gaining is giving. I must try this again and again; and I may expect that as much of prosperity as will be good for me will come to me as a gracious reward for a liberal course of action."[231]

Spurgeon made a connection between giving and financial prosperity: "I have noticed that the most generous Christians have always been the most happy and almost invariably the most prosperous. I have seen the liberal giver rise to wealth of which he never dreamed. . . . It takes faith to act toward our God with an open hand."[232] Similarly, A.B. Simpson, while emphasizing the importance of pure motives, taught, "Thus we gain by giving. Thus we possess twice over by letting go."[233] We rise to throne heights through our generous spirit of giving.

Stay Out of Debt. God's throne lacks nothing. God declared, "I own the cattle on a thousand hills." Therefore, if we are living Throne Life, we have no need to go into debt. George Müller testified that he and his wife never went into debt because they believed it to be unscriptural according to Romans 13:8. As a result, many trials afflict believers because they are not obeying this Scripture. Müller observed that God never promises that He will pay our debts. Hudson Taylor avowed, "God's work done in God's way will not lack God's support. He is just as able to supply funds ahead of time as afterward and He much prefers doing so."

Be Satisfied with What You Have. Hudson Taylor asserted, "The real secret of an unsatisfied life lies too often in an unsurrendered will."[234] Spurgeon wrote, "Happiness is not found when the barns are full and the vats are running over. Happiness is knowing that whatever you have, the Lord is your provider. You cannot have a better provider." His attitude toward wealth was, "Prayer makes 'rich toward God,' and this is the best of riches." [235] Simpson believed the key to receiving blessing from God is: "When you become satisfied with God, everything else so loses its charm that He can give it to you without harm, and then you can take just as much as you choose, and use it for His glory. . . . Then every bank stock, and investment will be but a channel through which you can pour out His benevolence and share His gifts."[236] Contentment is thus a key to true prosperity.

The basic problem is not whether God desires to prosper believers, but rather how prosperity is defined. We should look to these giants of faith as models through their characteristically simple, frugal, self-denying lives.

God does want His people to prosper, to have everything we need in order to sufficiently accomplish all He desires. God does not want His people to be involuntarily impoverished. Yet the motives and goals for prosperity must be pure and Spirit-led.

I would encourage those who are seeking prosperity to have the "holy indifference" toward wealth that the classic faith leaders advocated and modeled. They show us that we need to be content and moderate, not extravagant and self-indulgent. We must understand that in some situations God may want us to humble ourselves to the lowest, and in others it may be entirely appropriate for us to go first class.

We should not assume that God always wants us to seek the best and finest in comfort and luxury, but neither should we assume that God always wants us to take the cheapest way. Seeking God's desire for the situation should be our desire. The classic faith leaders caution us that it is possible to focus so much on the material blessings that one can miss the greater blessings, which, ultimately, are not material.

True Throne Life maintains a "holy indifference" to physical prosperity. John Oxenham expresses this poetically:

Better in bitterest agony to lie,
Before Thy throne,
Than through much increase to be lifted up on high,
And stand alone.

Yet best—the need that broke me at Thy feet,
In voiceless prayer,
And cast my chastened heart, a sacrifice complete,
Upon Thy care.

Trust God, Taking Your Needs to Him, Not to Others. This concept Müller practiced and passed on to Taylor, Simpson, Spurgeon, Carmichael, and others, as with his principle on owing no debts. Amy Carmichael explained, "We do not tell when we are in need unless definitely asked, and even then not always; for often the leading seems to be silent, except towards God."[237] Who is showing greater faith? Those who plead for funds, or those who do not broadcast their needs? The greatest demonstration of faith—throne faith—is to pray and trust God to provide without telling others.

Pray and Believe for Abundance. Many of the classic faith leaders believed in the concept of multi-fold increase. Commenting on the feeding of the 5,000, Amy Carmichael testified, "And, as I believed, the promise was given to me then that there should be baskets over and above our daily supplies."[238] She understood that as we give of ourselves to others, by God's grace He will provide abundantly from the leftovers. Hudson Taylor trusted that God would provide even ten times over. Oswald Chambers testified that whenever he gave sacrificially, God doubled: "The Lord always gives double for all I give away." They did not, however, like some contemporary faith teaching make a formula for obtaining a hundred-fold increase.

Make Specific Requests. Müller would paraphrase James 4:1 to say, "You have not *exactly* what you need because you asked not for *exactly* what you needed." He believed that vague prayers get vague answers; specific prayers get specific answers. Müller prayed for precise amounts of money, and again and again would receive exactly what he needed. For instance, one time he asked the Lord for a thousand pounds of money, and he received varying amounts from one shilling to a hundred pounds from several sources totaling exactly that amount.

Also, he asked that the Lord would place on the hearts of people to donate time and articles of furniture and clothes for the children. As a result, he received every item he needed, plus food, volunteers to care for the children, and an offer of a house! Sometimes it took long periods of time, but he continued to pray repeatedly with precision. For one particular need, he prayed specifically for 134 days before receiving the answer.

Claim Throne Provision and Prosperity. When we are in the will of God and have that holy indifference to wealth, we can claim with humble, selfless boldness the prosperity and provision God desires for His kingdom throne work to be accomplished. Sarah Foulkes Moore encourages us to exercise the authority of the believer to claim throne provision:

> The same authority is available in its exercise of releasing funds for the advancement of Christian work. Satan is hindering Christian enterprise by tying up funds. Believers have the power to unite and agree that these barriers to Christian benevolence give way. Men and women of faith, courage, and determination need to rise in the Church and bind these hostile forces, garrisoned against the financial prosperity of the world-wide advance of the Gospel. A Christian worker whose ministry was suffering for funds, finding her prayers for God's provision unanswered, rebuked the poverty demon and bound the satanic hindrance to prayer. Each time her funds were held up, she exercised this authority in union with Christ and released funds for her blessed work for the Master. In these perilous days, the powers of darkness conscious of their impending overthrow, are fiercely resisting on all fronts, so much so that every prayer upward needs resistance Satanward to prevail."

For Reflection

1. In what ways have you experienced throne prosperity?

2. What hinders you from experiencing throne prosperity more fully?

3. Which of the principles of throne prosperity is the most meaningful to you and why?

CHAPTER 15

Throne Holiness

"God sits upon the throne of His holiness" (Ps 47:8, NKJV).

The Holy of Holies is the Throne of God. Therefore, the throne of God is characterized by holiness. God sits upon a throne of holiness. You cannot sit with Jesus in the heavenly places without a profound holiness coming upon you and invading your life. If you are living Throne Life, you will be living a holy life. If you are not walking in throne holiness, you are not living Throne Life.

The Awesome Experience of Throne Holiness

Isaiah writes of his own dramatic experience of his eyes being opened to the heavenly temple and seeing the splendor of God's holiness and glory: "I saw the Lord sitting upon a throne, lofty and exalted, with the train of His robe filling the temple. Seraphim stood above Him. . . . And one called out to another and said, Holy, Holy, Holy is the Lord of hosts, the whole earth is full of His glory" (Isa 6:1, 2a, 3).

Throne Holiness Shakes Our Foundations. After seeing the vision of God on the throne in the temple and the seraphim declaring the holiness and glory of God, Isaiah records that he was shaken:

"And the foundations of the thresholds trembled at the voice of him who called out, while the temple was filling with smoke" (Isa 6:4). Having a revelation of God on His throne will shake the very foundations of our lives. The author of Hebrews writes of "the removing of those things which can be shaken, as of created things, so that those things which cannot be shaken may remain" (Heb 12:27). Holiness sifts out anything that is not secure on the Rock of Christ, so that "we receive a kingdom which cannot be shaken" (Heb 12:28).

Throne Holiness Humbles Us. Our first response when we enter the Holy of Holies is that of Isaiah, "Woe is me, for I am ruined! Because I am a man of unclean lips" (Isa 6:5). Even though we are welcomed to share in Christ's throne, we have an overwhelming sense of our unworthiness apart from Christ. When we see God as He really is, we see ourselves as we really are apart from Christ— broken, and torn, and in shambles. It is a broken, contrite heart that enables us to rise to holy throne heights. A.W. Tozer explains, "He may be and often is highest when he feels lowest and most sinless when he is most conscious of sin."[239]

Tozer understands that the way up is down. The way to throne rights and authority is holy surrender: "Let no one imagine that he will lose anything of human dignity by this voluntary sell-out of his all to his God. He does not by this degrade himself as a man; rather he finds his right place of high honor as one made in the image of his Creator. . . . In exalting God over all he finds his own highest honor upheld."[240]

Throne Holiness Purifies Us. George Watson describes the role of purity in relation to the throne and the kingdom of God: "Purity reveals Jesus to me as my heaven-enthroned and heart-enthroned King. Pardon places me in the kingdom of God; purity places the kingdom of God in me."[241] Theologically, this is the difference between *imputed* righteousness and *imparted* righteousness. When we are born again, righteousness is imputed, that is, reckoned, to us. We are clothed in the righteousness of Christ. We are declared to be "saints," holy ones. Purification then imparts holiness within us.

When we are born again, we begin kingdom life. However, we have no inheritance in the kingdom of God without purity (Eph 5:3-5). Purity empowers us to receive and enjoy our kingdom inheritance from the throne of God. We find three images of purification in Scripture: 1) purification through fire, 2) cleansing through water, 3) purging through pruning.

Holiness will come to us as fire from the throne, "for our God is a consuming fire" (Heb 12:29). Fire burns out all alloy, all impurities, all that is unlike life at the throne. Just as fire separates the dross from the pure gold, so holy fire will come as separation from all that is unclean, from all that is less than holy. Job proclaims in the midst of his fiery trial, "When He has tried me, I shall come forth as [pure] gold" (Job 23:10). Five different Hebrew words are used for "gold" in the book of Job. The word Job uses here means pure gleaming gold, gold refined in the fire. When we experience throne holiness, we become like pure, 24-karat gold, gleaming with the glory of God.

Holiness will also come as pure, cleansing water flowing. At the throne of God, uncleanness is non-existent. Pure water flows from the throne of God to purify any uncleanness in our lives. We are washed clean through the word of God (Eph 5:26).

Finally, holiness purifies through purging out the dead, unfruitful branches in our lives. "You are already clean [pruned, purged] because of the word which I have spoken to you" (John 15:2). No deadness exists at the throne of God, except for deadness to self. Throne Life is full of fruit-bearing. Pruning is painful, but the effects of pruning are bearing more fruit, much fruit, abiding fruit.

Throne Holiness Raises Us to Throne Position. Elihu, speaking to Job in behalf of God, encourages Job that the righteous who are afflicted will be raised to the throne:

> He does not withdraw His eyes from the righteous;
> But with kings on the throne
> He has seated them forever, and they are exalted (Job 36:7).

Likewise, Isaiah prophesies that the righteous will be raised to the heights:

> He who walks righteously and speaks with sincerity,
> He who rejects unjust gain
> And shakes his hands so that they hold no bribe;
> He who stops His ears from hearing about bloodshed
> And shuts his eyes from looking upon evil;
> He will dwell on the heights,
> His refuge will be with the impregnable rock;
> His bread will be given him,
> His water will be sure.
> Your eyes will see the King in His beauty (Isa 33:15-17a).

George Watson describes the role of holiness to raise us to the heights: "Pardon and purity are the two wings on which perfect love can soar and sing its way to the high mountain of God."[242] Holiness empowers us to soar to the heavenly mountaintops with God.

Throne Holiness Lifts Us Above Sin. A.B. Simpson taught the law of lift overcoming the law of gravity spiritually, even before the laws of aerodynamics were understood:

> There is a stronger law than the law of gravitation—my own life and will. So through the operation of this higher law— the law of my vitality—I defy the law of gravitation, and lift my hand and hold it above its former resting place and move it at my will. The law of vitality has made me free from the law of gravitation.

> Precisely so the indwelling life of Christ Jesus, operating with the power of the law lifts me above and counteracts the power of sin in my fallen nature. This is the secret of sanctification. It is not so much the expulsion of sin, as the incoming of the Holy Spirit, which has broken the control which sin formerly exercised, lifting me into an entirely new sphere of holy life and victory.[243]

Throne Holiness Elevates Our Faith. A.B. Simpson asserted that holiness is essential for walking by faith: "Faith requires for its heavenly vision the highlands of holiness and separation, the pure sky of a consecrated life."[244] Think of that—the pure sky of a consecrated life! Often our vision is impeded by dust clouds of doubt and impurity. However, when we have a consecrated life, we are seated on the throne in the heavenlies, and we can see forever.

Throne Holiness Radiates God's Glory in Our Face. Thomas Watson describes the life that characterizes throne holiness:

> Our deportment is in heaven; we walk as nobles of that city. . . . A godly Christian should be known by his face—his life should show that he is going to the Jerusalem above. A true saint is a citizen of heaven; he manifests what place he belongs to—by his speech, habits, and walk. There is a kind of angelic brightness on him; he shines in holiness, as Moses' face shined when he had been with God in the mount. He is still doing angels' work—his life is a very heaven upon earth. [245]

Holiness is noble. When we walk in holiness, we will exemplify nobility. Angelic brightness describes how others see you when you are living the holiness of Throne Life.

How to Live Throne Holiness

Throne Holiness Is Christ's Work, Not Ours. It is vital that we understand that throne holiness is the Christ life, the life of Christ producing holiness in us, not our own effort. A.B. Simpson explains:

> The resurrection of Christ is the power that sanctifies us. It enables us to count our old life, our former self, annihilated, so that we are no longer the same person in the eyes of God, or of ourselves; and we may with confidence repudiate ourselves and refuse either to obey or fear our former evil nature. Indeed, it is the risen Christ Himself who comes to

dwell within us, and becomes in us the power of this new life and victorious obedience. It is not merely the fact of the resurrection, but the fellowship of the Risen One that brings us our victory and our power. We have learned the meaning of the sublime paradox, "I am crucified with Christ: nevertheless I live; yet not I, but Christ liveth in me." This is the only true and lasting sanctification, the indwelling life of Christ, the Risen One, in the believing and obedient soul.[246]

Paul describes in 2 Corinthians 6:16-7:1 how to live throne holiness. We first need to recognize, as we explained in Chapter 2 that "we are the temple of the living God" (verse 16a). We are the sacred sanctuary of the throne of God, the dwelling place of God: "I will dwell in them and walk among them" (verse 16b). Once we understand our position of throne holiness, we can live it out through the following steps.

Set Yourself Apart <u>to God</u> as His Own. "'And I will be their God, and they shall be My people. . . . And I will be a father to you, and you shall be sons and daughters to Me,' says the Lord Almighty" (verses 16c, 18). God has adopted us as His sons and daughters. We are His own. We have been elevated and set apart by God as royalty, as His chosen people. He has set us apart to Him as His treasured possession: "You shall be My own possession [special treasure] among all the peoples" (Ex 19:5).

So then, we reciprocate and set ourselves apart in covenant relationship with Him. In the traditional marriage vows, we pledge to keep our self only for our spouse, "forsaking all others." So likewise, we pledge to keep ourselves only for God, forsaking all others. In so doing, we dedicate ourselves to God: "Therefore, I urge you, brethren, by the mercies of God, to present your bodies a living and holy sacrifice, acceptable to God, which is your spiritual service of worship" (Rom 12:1). Presenting ourselves as a sacrifice prepares us to enter the Holy of Holies, the throne room of God.

Set Yourself Apart from the World and Sin. Because we want to please God, we separate ourselves from all that is unclean, from all that would displease the One we love: "'Therefore, come out from their midst and be separate,' says the Lord. 'And do not touch what is unclean; and I will welcome you'" (verse 17). No dirt is found in God's throne room, no uncleanness in the Holiest of Holies. This is not a matter of legalism with a list of do's and don't's, but a matter of desiring the very best of what God wants for us and removing anything that might hinder our intimacy with God. We cannot live the fullness of Throne Life until we separate ourselves from the world and sin.

Cleanse Yourself Daily. "Therefore, having these promises, beloved, let us cleanse ourselves from all defilement of flesh and spirit. . ." (7:1a). We are purified, as mentioned above, by the water of the Word (Eph 5:25-26), by the fire of the Holy Spirit (Luke 3:16-17; 1 Pet 1:6-7), and by the pruning work of the Word (John 15:1-2). We need daily cleansing because we encounter the slime of life daily and need a cleansing bath. As we humbly and intentionally present ourselves to God every day, asking Him to cleanse us, He washes us and prunes us with His Word and burns out of our lives the dross that clings to us.

We might think, "Well, I understand how my flesh might need a daily cleansing, but why my spirit? Isn't my spirit already clean?" True it is that our spirits have been made pure, for the Holy Spirit dwells within our human spirit and we become partakers of His divine nature (2 Pet 1:4).

It is not our spirit within that needs to be cleansed, but the dirt and grime and sludge that cover and encase our spirit. Unless we have a daily cleansing, a greasy film forms over our spirit, which then hardens and forms a shell that needs to be broken. Watchman Nee explains, "The shell of the outward man must be smashed by God. The more it is shattered, the more the life in the spirit is released. As long as this shell remains intact, the burden in the spirit cannot be released, nor can God's life and power flow from you to the Church."[247]

Receive Impartation of Christ's Character Within. "... perfecting <u>holiness</u> in the fear of God" (7:1b). Holiness is the character of Christ. As we are made holy, we are not only clothed with His righteousness, but His righteousness becomes internalized within us and is manifested from us. As we fear Him (not in the sense of being afraid, but rather reverence), His wisdom is imparted to us, for "the fear of the Lord, that is wisdom" (Job 28:28). As we abide in Christ our vine, we bear fruit, the fruit of the Spirit, which is the very character of Christ. As His character is formed within us, we not only reflect His glory, but we radiate His glory from within us.

Be Made Whole. "... <u>*perfecting*</u> holiness in the fear of God" (7:1b). The Greek word for "perfect" means to make complete, whole, to finish the goal. Paul explains further, "Now may the God of peace Himself sanctify you entirely; and may your spirit and soul and body be preserved complete, without blame at the coming of our Lord Jesus Christ" (1 Thess 5:23). Based on this, A.B. Simpson's motto was, "Holiness is wholeness." When we are holy, we are made whole. Throne Life is a whole life, a life that is complete, harmonious, all that God intends.

To be wholly sanctified, Simpson explains, does not mean sinless perfection. Rather, it means that our whole being—body, soul, and spirit—experiences the transforming, sanctifying power of the Holy Spirit. To be wholly sanctified practically means that our understanding, our tastes, our affections and passions, our appetites, our talents, our ambitions, our lips, our hands, our feet, our eyes, our ears are made holy, befitting our position at the throne of God.

The Practical Possibilities of Throne Holiness

Ultimately, throne holiness is a high estate of nobility and integrity, in which we walk in regal splendor with heavenly possibilities. In his classic book *Wholly Sanctified*, A.B. Simpson describes the majesty of throne holiness:

★ The Holy Spirit is a quickening force to a consecrated intellect. Minds that have been dull and obscure before have risen beneath His touch to the highest intellectual attainments and the mightiest achievements of human genius. . . .

★ A consecrated body . . . has learned to regard every sense and organ, not as a minister of our own pleasure, but a channel for His life and a weapon for His work. . . .

★ Consecrated ears will be very attentive to all He would have us hear, as well as dead to other voices.

★ Consecrated eyes will see a thousand opportunities which others pass by unheeded, a thousand beauties and meaning in things which others miss.

★ Consecrated feet will find the path of duty always easy; the highest stairs, the most lonely walks, the most repulsive journeys, the most self-denying tasks a willing service for their Lord. . . .

★ A consecrated voice will have a new power to sing and speak. . . .

★ A sanctified body . . . will carry us above our physical infirmities on the high tide of a supernatural vitality, which is not dependent upon our organic conditions, but elevates us above them and becomes a heavenly nourishment to all our conscious life and work.

Let us arise to our potential through holiness!

For Reflection

1. What aspect of throne holiness is missing from your life? How can you experience throne holiness in that area?

2. How is God working out holiness in your life—through the cleansing water of the Word, through purifying fire, through pruning?

3. What part of your being is God calling you to consecrate to Him?

CHAPTER 16

Throne Health and Healing

"Who pardons all your iniquities, who heals all your diseases"
(Ps 103:3).

"By His scourging we are healed" (Isa 53:5; 1 Pet 2:24).

"And as you go, preach, saying, 'The kingdom of heaven is at
hand.' Heal the sick, raise the dead, cleanse the lepers, cast out
demons. Freely you received, freely give" (Matt 10:7-8).

Health and healing are characteristic of the Kingdom of God.
Jesus declared that when the kingdom of heaven is at hand,
the sick are healed, the lepers are cleansed, the dead are raised,
demons are cast out. And He instructed us to pray, "Your kingdom
come, Your will be done on earth as it is in heaven." There is no sickness in heaven, no sickness at the throne of God. So when we pray
for God's kingdom to come on earth, we are praying for kingdom
health and healing to come on earth.

The Children's Bread

People debate over whether or not healing is in the atonement.
Some say no, it is not. Others say, yes it is, and it is guaranteed,

implying that those who are not healed must either lack in faith or are in sin. Both extremes fail to take into account that the kingdom of God is both here now, but not yet fully here.

One of the privileges of Throne Life is throne health and healing, the foretaste of the heavenly life in the here-and-now. George Peck encourages us as believers to "discern in the resurrection of Christ's physical body. . . . the privilege now available to his faith, in view of his present identification with Christ's glorified body. "

When we experience Throne Life, we can experience throne health and healing. Although seldom do we experience total health and healing in this life, the more we live out Throne Life, the more we can actualize throne health.

Sickness does not exist in the heavenly places. So in the spirit, in the heavenly places, from the perspective of the throne, by Jesus' wounds, yes, we have been healed and we are healed. Jesus instructs us to pray, "Thy kingdom come, Thy will be done, on earth as it is in heaven." When Jesus' kingdom comes on earth, heavenly healing is imparted. Jesus further declared, "But if I cast out demons by the Spirit of God, then the kingdom of God has come upon you" (Matt. 12:28). Kingdom healing is throne healing. Kingdom health is throne health.

From the throne perspective we have been healed. When we view ourselves from the throne, we can see our healing even if we do not see it manifested on earth. When we pray, "Thy Kingdom come, thy will be done on earth as it is in heaven, we are praying for throne health and healing to come.

Divine healing, Jesus declared to the Canaanite woman, is the "children's bread," or as Keith Bailey explains, "the blessing of physical healing by divine intervention was the unique privilege of a covenant people in proper relationship to God."[248] It is the privilege of the child of God, a provision of Jesus' atonement for our sins.

Throne Health Is Related to Throne Holiness. Andrew Murray explains, "True salvation and true health consist in being holy as God is holy."[249] Life on the throne of God is wholeness. When we are living that life, we are whole. As mentioned in the last chapter, A.B. Simpson explains, 'A sanctified body . . . will carry us above our physical infirmities on the high tide of a supernatural vitality, which is not dependent upon our organic conditions, but elevates us above them and becomes a heavenly nourishment to all our conscious life and work."

Throne Health Includes All God's Healing Arsenal. God uses a wide array of resources from the throne to bring health and healing—supernatural healing, gifts of healing, confession of the Word, the Lord's Supper, healthy living, nutrition, medicine and doctors, and the list goes on. To live throne health does not mean to abandon doctors and medicine.

Simpson provides an apt summary of the Higher Life view of healing, which is sound counsel for today: "Divine Healing is not giving up medicines, or fighting with physicians, or against remedies. It is not even believing in prayer, or the prayer of faith, or in the men and women who teach Divine Healing. . . . But it is really receiving the personal life of Christ to be in us as the supernatural strength of our body, and the supply of our life."[250]

At the same time, many who live out Throne Life have discovered keys to health and healing and have received faith from the very throne of God to trust God without medicine. A.B. Simpson, Andrew Murray, C.T. Studd, and Rees Howells were some who amazingly experienced throne health with little or no use of medicine. They advised not to abandon medicine unless God imparts the very faith of God to do so.

Throne Health Provides Strength in Weakness. A.B. Simpson assures us that God can "endue us with the power to resist disease, to persevere under the influence of a harsh climate, to endure hardship and suffering and to go through life, like Moses, with unabated strength until our work is finished." He also wrote with insight of some who have not received divine healing, but receive strength in their infirmities:

> Yet such persons daily experience a supernatural quickening of their bodies which gives them freshness and strength and in some instances extraordinary physical endurance. Indeed, they seem to have something more than Divine Healing; they have Divine Life. Theirs indeed is a paradoxical experience. Instead of being bedridden or helpless invalids they keep going in the strength of Jesus, not only carrying their own burdens but stretching out a helping hand to others. Surely it is one thing to sink down under the power of disease or the weight of infirmity; but it is quite another thing to rise above the power of disease and the weight of infirmity and in the strength of the ascended and glorified Christ not only have a victorious spirit but bear fruit, yea, the 'much fruit' that shall abide the day of His coming.[251]

Throne Health Means You Are Immortal Until Your Work Is Done. Higher Life leaders affirmed that if we are walking in the will of God and in obedience to God, we cannot die before our time. Spurgeon claimed this principle during the great cholera plague in London about 1855:

> One day, sick in heart, walking dejectedly down Great Dover Road on his way home from another funeral, he stopped and looked into an apothecary shop window. The shopkeeper, being a believer, had placed a placard in his window with a Scripture verse that read: "Because thou hast made the Lord, which is my refuge, even the Most High, thy habitation; there shall no evil befall thee neither shall any plague come nigh thy dwelling" (Ps 91:9). Immediately, the Spirit of God impressed the truth on Charles' heart. He claimed the promise as his own. Dramatically he came out of his depression and went about his work completely confident God would care for him and keep him safe from the plague. The lines of an old hymn

spoke to him: "Not a single shaft can hit, till the God of love sees fit." He remembered Cromwell's word, *"Man is immortal till his work is done."*[252]

A.B. Simpson expressed this principle as applied to the aging process: "The system might just wear out and pass away as naturally as the apple ripens and falls in autumn, or the wheat matures and dies. It has simply fulfilled its natural period. . . . The promise of healing is not physical immortality, but *health until our life work is done.*"[253]

At the same time, Simpson understood that this is an ideal and does not mean that a person never age: "The Word places a limit to human life, and all that Scriptural faith can claim is sufficiency of health and strength for our life-work and within its fair limits."[254] Ahijah was a prophet of God who had become blind through old age, yet operated in the supernatural gifts of prophecy and word of knowledge (1 Kings 14:4-5). Elisha performed many miracles, including raising the dead, but died of a sickness. Even more surprising, after his death, a dead man came back to life when his body touched Elisha's grave.

Experiencing Throne Life in Death. Simpson recognized, that in many cases when healing does not occur, it is not a deficiency of faith, but rather that God has not imparted special faith for healing. A double portion of the Spirit rested upon Elisha, a great man of faith. Regarding his death, Simpson remarked, "His faith might easily have claimed exemption from his last illness, and possibly even from death itself, but like his great Master of whom he was the especial type, in all things he was made like unto his brethren, that he might teach us the faith that could glorify God, both in life and death. . . . All that was evil and of the enemy in connection with his illness was eliminated by the power of God, for we find his faith in the freest and fullest exercise, even on his dying couch. . . . We cannot doubt that a faith so mighty could easily have claimed his own recovery. But his work was done."[255]

Simpson recognized a dignity in dying of an illness that some fail to comprehend: "It is a beautiful picture of faith that even infirmity and approaching dissolution cannot subdue or even cloud, reminding us that the Christian's last hours may be his brightest and that the sublimest triumphs of his life should be in the face even of his foes. Have we not all seen such victories, the withering frame and worn out forces of nature . . . and the very frailty of the outward temple made it more transparent to the glory that was shining out from within, while the walls were crumbling into decay and the inward guest was fluttering for its flight to a brighter sphere?"[256]

So be of good courage, dying of an illness may not be lack of faith, but may actually be the exercise of great faith.

Living Throne Health and Healing

Maintain a Joyful Spirit. A.B. Simpson counseled: "A flash of ill temper, a cloud of despondency, an impure thought or desire can poison your blood, inflame your tissues, disturb your nerves and interrupt the whole process of God's life in your body! On the other hand, the spirit of joy, freedom from anxious care and worry, a generous and loving heart, the sedative of peace, the uplifting influence of hope and confidence—these are better than pills, stimulants and sedatives, and the very nature of things will exercise the most benign influence over your physical functions, making it true in a literal as well as a spiritual sense, that 'the joy of the Lord is your strength.'"[257]

Spurgeon also advised, "Let your conscious feebleness provoke you to seek the means of strength: and that means of strength is to be found in a pleasant medicine, sweet as it is profitable—the delicious and effectual medicine of 'the joy of the Lord.'"[258]

Simpson, referring to Proverbs 17:22, counseled out of his own experience, "Joy is the great restorer and healer. Gladness of spirit will bring health to the bones and vitality to the nerves when all other tonics fail, and all other sedatives cease to quiet. Sick one, begin to rejoice in the Lord, and your bones will flourish like an herb, and your cheeks will glow with the bloom of health and freshness. . . . Joy is balm and healing; and if you will but rejoice, God will give power."[259]

Activate a Positive Mental Attitude. S.D. Gordon used the term "right mental attitude" in relation to health and healing, meaning that we are thinking on Christ, not our circumstances: "A right mental attitude exerts enormous influence. . . . Incidently, this is the process of faith at work, a simple faith in Christ, in-breathed by the Holy Spirit. The objective mind lays hold of Christ's promises and accepts unquestioningly the result as already assured."[260] Gordon wrote, "That mental attitude [thinking on Christ] will vitally and radically affect your body."[261]

Hudson Taylor exhorts us to focus our mind on Christ: "How then to have our faith increased? Only by thinking of all that Jesus is and all He is for us: His life, His death, His work, He Himself as revealed to us in the Word to be the subject of our constant thought."[262] Thus the classic faith writers taught that a positive mental attitude *can* affect one's health and outcome of life. However, it is not by our own mental effort, but by letting our thoughts dwell on Jesus and His Word.

Cultivate an Atmosphere of Faith. The concept of faith homes developed by Johann Blumhardt, Dorothea Trudel, A.B. Simpson, Carrie Judd Montgomery, and others in the 1800s, was intended to provide a positive atmosphere of faith in which a person could receive healing, not unlike today's retreat centers. Kelso Carter indicates that more than thirty faith homes had been established in the latter part of the nineteenth century. Andrew Murray was healed after spending three weeks at Elizabeth Baxter's Bethshan Home in London. Montgomery founded "Faith Rest Cottage," explaining, "The peace and quietness which pervade our little Home, and communion with those of like precious faith, will often aid the dear, struggling ones to come into the place of victory."[263]

Soak in God's Word. Andrew Murray believed in the creative power of the Scriptures to produce health and strength: "Let the Word create around you, create within you a holy atmosphere, a holy, heavenly light, in which your soul will be refreshed and strengthened for the work of daily life."[264]

Simpson's friend, Wheaton College president Charles Blanchard, wrote of the healing power of Scripture, describing how a physician prescribed to a depressed, nervous, sick woman to read the Bible an hour for thirty days then come back and see him. She eventually obtained an appetite for the Word and came back to the doctor a different woman. He told her, "I saw as soon as you came into the room that what you needed was not medicine nor anything else that man could give or do. What you needed was God. You have now come in touch with Him. Keep in touch with Him and you will be well."

To Müller, renewing and strengthening this positive attitude of the inner man daily is an essential prerequisite to witnessing and helping others in the right spirit. He accomplished this by establishing a habit of walking and meditating on the Word of God before breakfast each morning. Considering it food as nourishment for the inner man, Müller claimed this practice was also beneficial to his health. His own testimony after forty years of this faith walk was: "I cannot tell you how happy this service makes me. Instead of being the anxious, careworn man many persons think me to be, I have no anxieties and no cares at all. Faith in God leads me to roll all my burdens upon Him." One of his biographers, Roger Steer, noted, "Müller's longevity (he died when he was ninety-two) surely confirms his insistence that he was not worn out by worry."[265]

Avoid Negative Attitudes of Fear, Doubt, and Anxiety. Just as a positive mental attitude may result in positive effects such as healing, so negative attitudes may result in negative effects. The 17th century French archbishop Fenelon, precursor of Higher Life thinking, warned about the consequences of a negative mental attitude: "The strivings of the human mind not only impair the health of your body, but also bring dryness to the soul. You can actually consume yourself by too much inner striving. . . . Your peace and inner sweetness can be destroyed by a restless mind."[266]

Hannah Whitall Smith, influenced by Fenelon, expanded upon his thought: "A desponding person is apt to fail in everything he undertakes, while a cheerful, courageous person seems to succeed without any effort. Our mental conditions are far more powerful to affect material things than we know, and I believe that there is here a secret of enormous power, if human beings once understood it." She wrote out of personal experience with her husband's nervous breakdowns and doubts, leading to his loss of faith.

Charles Spurgeon suffered much pain from his gout and fell into deep depressions, but also found the importance of this principle, testifying, "Worry kills, but confidence in God is like healing medicine."[267] Spurgeon's friend F.B. Meyer avowed that negative thinking can even cause illness: "The healthiest people do not think about their health; the weak induce disease by morbid introspection."[268] Moreover, Simpson warned, "Worry, fear, distrust, care—all are poisonous!"[269]

Expect Health and Healing. For Simpson, an optimistic attitude, rather than pessimism, can have a positive effect on health. In his pamphlet *How To Receive Divine Healing*, he counseled not to expect sickness: "Don't expect to have a spell of weariness and reaction," but rather "just go calmly forward, . . . expecting Him to give you the necessary strength to carry you thru [sic]."

Maintain Assurance Even with Negative Symptoms. Carrie Montgomery asserted that once a person has heard from the Lord, "If the Devil brings his symptoms, *when the Lord has declared you to be free,* if he tries to put his tags of different diseases upon you, you have a right to refuse those tags."

Ultimately, Look to Jesus for Health and Healing. Higher Life healing pioneer Charles Cullis gives us timeless counsel: "The promises are revealed to those who are 'looking unto Jesus.'. . . If you are constantly 'looking unto Jesus,' you will be kept in perfect peace and safety." Early Methodist leader Hester Ann Rogers testified of such throne health: "By constantly looking to Jesus, I receive fresh strength in every time of need."

You, too, can receive strength, health, and healing from the throne!

For Reflection

1. In what ways can you live in a greater way throne health and healing?

2. What obstacles keep you from experiencing throne health and healing?

CHAPTER 17

Throne Heights— Going Still Higher

"I press on . . ." (Phil 3:14a).

Don't Be Satisfied with the Higher Life

Throne heights are the *upper* regions of the heavenly places. George Peck bids us to reach for the throne heights: "There are two regions in the heavenlies, one above where the evil spirits have the power to attack us, and one where we are seated with Him on the throne far above all principalities and powers. It is possible for us to be rid of the dominion of the flesh and the devil. If we abide in Jesus, and He in us by the Holy Ghost, we shall know of His being in us as the resurrected and also as the enthroned one. We should be seated there with Him, and not wrestling with the devil. . . . Friends, don't be satisfied with the higher life; but take the highest."

No matter how far or how high we have gone in Christ, there is so much more. The sequel to Oswald Chambers' classic devotional book, *My Utmost for His Highest*, is entitled *Still Higher for His Highest*. He recognized our need to keep pressing on. I remember in one of Kathryn Kuhlman's meetings, in which she said, "It is great to be baptized with the Holy Spirit, but there is so much more." In other words, no matter how many or how great your experiences of Throne Life, press on for more of God. No matter how much we have entered into the Holy of Holies, we are still on the outskirts, still on the fringes of the holiest and most heavenly.

Jesus Calls Us Even Higher—
to the Mount of Transfiguration

"Jesus took with Him Peter and James and John his brother, and led [anaphero—to lead up higher] them up on a high mountain by themselves"(Matt. 17:1).

Not everyone reaches those heights, even though everyone can. Only Peter, James, and John were carried into the Almighty Presence on the Mount of Transfiguration. He will take us there when we are ready. Even Peter, James, and John, the inner circle of Jesus, did not know what to do or how to act when they came to the mount. They understood that this was something special, something sacred, a climactic experience. Yet they could not conceive how special, how sacred, how climactic.

No matter what heights we have attained, God bids us come up even higher. As C.S. Lewis portrays it in his book *The Last Battle* in *The Chronicles of Narnia* series, "further up and further in." There is no plateau in the Christian life. Oswald Chambers highlights that God is calling us ever higher:

A higher state of mind and spiritual vision can only be achieved through the higher practice of personal character. If you live up to the highest and best that you know in the outer level of your life, God will continually say to you, "Friend, come up even higher."

. . . Compare this week in your spiritual life with the same week last year to see how God has called you to a higher level. We have all been brought to see from a higher viewpoint. Never allow God to show you a truth which you do not instantly begin to live up to, applying it to your life. Always work through it, staying in its light. . . . Have you heard God say, "Come up higher," not audibly on the outer level, but to the innermost part of your character?[270]

Receive Fresh Manifestations, New Visitations

If we get to the place where we think we have arrived, that we have no more to learn, no more to experience, we will stagnate in our Christian life. Charles Spurgeon urges us still higher to fresh visitations from God:

No matter what level of spiritual maturity we are on, we need renewed appearances, fresh manifestations, new visitations from on high. While it is right to thank God for the past and look back with joy to His visits to you in your early days as a believer, I encourage you to seek God for special visitations of His presence. . . . Consider that though the ocean has its high tides twice every day, yet it also has its spring tides. The sun shines whether we see it or not, even through our winter's fog, and yet it has its summer brightness. If we walk with God constantly, there are special seasons when He opens the very secret of His heart to us and manifests Himself to us – not only as He does not to the world but also as He does not at all times to His own favored ones. Not every day in a palace is a banqueting day, and not all days with God are so clear and glorious as certain special sabbaths of the soul in which the Lord unveils His glory.[271]

Seek God's Second Appearances

Again, referring to God's second appearance to Solomon at Gibeon, Spurgeon urges us on to seek "God's second appearances":

> We should be crying to God most pleadingly that He would speak to us a second time. . . . If the Lord has kept us steadfast in His fear, we are already possessors of what some call the higher life. This we are privileged to enjoy from the first hour of our spiritual life. We do not need to be converted again, but we do need the windows of heaven to be opened again and again over our heads. We need the Holy Spirit to be given again as at Pentecost and that we should renew our youth like the eagles, to run without weariness and walk without fainting.[272]

Third Heaven Experiences—Beyond Words

> *"I know a man in Christ who fourteen years ago—whether in the body I do not know, or out of the body I do not know, God knows—such a man was caught up to the third heaven.*
>
> *And I know how such a man . . . . was caught up into Paradise and heard inexpressible words, which a man is not permitted to speak" (2 Cor 12:2, 3a, 4).*

Being caught up to the third heaven is the apex of throne heights. Some people claim to have frequent third heaven experiences and flow easily in and out of the third heaven. However, this does not bear witness with Scripture. From Paul's description of being caught up into the third heaven, you can know you have had a third heaven experience when . . .

It Is a Rare Experience. The Apostle Paul experienced many visions and revelations. Yet he mentioned a third heaven experience only once. It was a rare occasion for Paul that went beyond the revelations, visions, and voices from God he had experienced.

The Spanish Christian mystic, Teresa of Avila, has perhaps been one of the few throughout church history who have experienced and understood such third heaven experiences. In Teresa's *Interior Castle*, she pictures seven mansions, in which a person progressively moves to the center or depths of God. The seventh mansion, being the most intimate dwelling place of God, would correspond to the third heaven of which Paul speaks. Teresa found that experiencing the seventh mansion in her castle was uncommon.

Contrary to Teresa and Paul, some people have claimed to be able to rise up into the third heaven easily and are dwelling in the third heaven constantly. If they really believe so, they have gone beyond the Apostle Paul and moved into Gnosticism. Because third heaven experiences by biblical example are exceptional, it is more likely that they are describing an experience of abiding in the presence of Christ, but not a third heaven experience.

Because those experiences of being caught up to the third heaven are infrequent in the lives of the greatest Christians, we cannot expect them frequently or seek to foster them. However, without seeking after them, as we pursue more of Jesus, He will take us higher into those heights.

You Don't Know Whether It Is an Out of the Body Experience. John Wesley's friend, Methodist theologian John Fletcher, described such an experience as a "supernatural discovery of the glory of God in an ineffable converse with Him face-to-face, so that whether in the body or out of the body, I cannot tell." Scottish theologian William Guthrie once told of an exceptional experience of the manifest presence of God as "a ray of glory filling the soul with God. . . in a transport. . . . such a glance of glory. . . . so swallowing him up that he forgets all things except the presence manifestation.""

You Don't Have Words to Express It. Such third heaven experiences involve spiritual insights that are unutterable. People who go around telling about their third heaven experiences, more likely than not, have not experienced a third heaven—certainly not the heights and depths of Paul's experience—or else they would not be able to talk about them. Dwight Moody gives us a glimpse of such an experience: "What a day, I cannot describe it. I seldom refer to it, . . . almost too sacred an experience to name. . . . Such an experience of love that I had to ask Him to stay His hand."

When we are transported into the high heavens, as Moody describes, it is almost too sacred, too holy, too divine to speak. Earthly words are not enough and are too ignoble for heavenly portrayal. As mentioned in Chapter 7, Andrew Murray once had a third heaven experience while commemorating the Lord's Supper. Yet he never mentioned it in his writings. We would never know of it, except for his daughter's recollection that a "deep solemnity" occurred for a time before he could speak.

A.W. Tozer also recognized that the heights and depths of the presence of God are beyond words:

> There are delights which the heart may enjoy in the awesome presence of God which cannot find expression in language; they belong to the unutterable element in Christian experience. . . . Some Christians are silent because they have nothing to say; others because what they have to say cannot be uttered by mortal tongue. . . . Where the Holy Spirit is permitted to exercise His full sway in a redeemed heart the progression is likely to be as follows: First, voluble praise, in prose speech or prayer or witness; then, when the crescendo rises beyond the ability of studied speech to express, comes song; when song breaks down under the weight of glory, then comes silence where the soul, held in deep fascination, feels itself blessed with an unutterable beatitude. [273]

Tozer goes on to explain the holiness and power of those unutterable moments: "More spiritual progress can be made in one short moment of speechless silence in the awesome presence of God than in years of mere study. While our mental powers are in command there is always the veil of nature between us and the face of God. It is only when our vaunted wisdom has been met and defeated in a breathless encounter with Omniscience that we are permitted really to know, when prostrate and wordless the soul receives divine knowledge like a flash of light on a sensitized plate. The exposure may be brief, but the results are permanent."[274]

You Are Humbled by the Experience. Some kind of a humbling experience goes hand-in-hand with the third heaven experience in order to prevent pride. Following his account of the revelation, he writes, "Because of the surpassing greatness of the revelations, for this reason, to keep me from exalting myself, there was given me a thorn in the flesh, a messenger of Satan to torment me—to keep me from exalting myself!" (2 Cor 12:7). Without getting into the debate over what the thorn in the flesh was, we can recognize that it was something that kept Paul humble. When we receive the greatest revelations, we will be humbled by them.

The great theologian Thomas Aquinas, who wrote his theological masterpiece *Summa Theologica*, near the end of his life had an "overwhelming direct experience of God," in which he received such overpowering revelations, so that he felt he could write no more. He intimated, "Such things have been revealed to me that all I have written seems as straw." His revelations convinced him that his great writings were only like straw. We wonder what it was that would bring him to that humbling conclusion. We wish he would have elaborated, but he was overwhelmed and wordless.

We also have just a glimpse of the experience of Jonathan Edwards, the great revivalist and one-time president of Princeton, "The glory of the Son of God appeared to me . . . full, pure, sweet grace and love. Ardency of soul, emptied and annihilated, to lie in the dust and to be full of Christ alone, perfectly sanctified and made pure."

When we do enter into the third heaven, we can say little. We are awed in the almighty, holy presence of God.

You Are Heavenly-Minded, Yet Remain Earthly-Grounded. An old saying goes, "Some people become so heavenly-minded that they are no earthly good." This can be a danger of throne height experiences. This does not mean that a person should not be heavenly-minded. Rather, that these higher experiences in the heavenlies should not isolate us from people or from serving the needs of others. God intends that we are so heavenly-minded that we are truly and fully earthly good. Puritan Thomas Brooks describes this heavenly-earthly union:

> A true saint is like the tribe of Manasseh, half of the tribe was on this side of the Jordan—and half on the other side in the *holy land*. So it is with a saint; half of him is on earth—and half in heaven! His flesh is on earth—his heart in heaven! As it was said of Paul, 2 Cor. 12:2, "Whether in the body I cannot tell, or whether out of the body I cannot tell;" so it may be said of a godly Christian, it is hard to tell whether he be in the body or out of the body! His love is in heaven, he is lodged in the tree of life. The fire of love boils the heart as high as heaven.

A.W. Tozer writes of the medieval theologian and mystic Meister Eckhart, that he "taught his followers that if they should find themselves in prayer as it were caught up to the third heavens and happen to remember that a poor widow needed food, they should break off the prayer instantly and go care for the widow. 'God will not suffer you to lose anything by it,' he told them. 'You can take up again in prayer where you left off and the Lord will make it up to you.' This is typical of the great mystics and masters of the interior life from Paul to the present day."[275]

Tozer, who himself experienced third heaven moments, shared of his own spiritual life, "I must testify that the highest, loftiest and most God-beholding moments in my own experience have been so calm that I could write about them, so peaceful that I could tell about them and analyze them."[276]

You Recognize That You Have Not Arrived. Fanny Crosby, the great blind hymn writer, seems to have approached third heaven experiences when she wrote in her beautiful hymn "Blessed Assurance": "perfect submission, perfect delight, visions of rapture now burst on my sight." She had amazing spiritual vision in spite of her physical blindness. Few have experienced her spiritual transport into the heights of heaven. Yet in her classic hymn "Draw Me Nearer," she penned words of holy yearning: "There are heights of joy that we may not reach until we rest in peace with Thee."

No matter how high and deep our experiences, no matter how amazing our revelations, there is so much more! Let us continue to press on to the heights of all God desires to do in us and reveal to us.

Conquering Self—The Highest Heights

Part of the "so much more" is the humility that involves conquering ourselves. A.W. Tozer once preached, "Before the kingdom of Christ can come in me, the kingdom of self must go out of me." If we want to reach the heights of Throne Life, more and more death to self will occur.

Thomas a Kempis, though writing centuries ago in his classic *The Imitation of Christ*, speaks timelessly and prophetically to us in the 21st century: "The perfect victory is to triumph over ourselves. For he who keeps himself subject in such a way that his sensual affections be obedient to reason, and his reason in all things obedient to Me; that person is truly conqueror of himself, and lord of the world. If you desire to mount to this height, you must set out courageously, and lay the axe to the root."

I encourage you to take up the ancient challenge of Thomas— courageously lay the axe to the root of yourself, and mount up to the heights of Throne Life. Keep pressing on for more and more of God Himself!

Throne Heights for the Church Universal

As I mentioned at the beginning of the book, we dream of the day when the entire church of Jesus Christ would catch the vision of the highest Christian life. It would transform and unite the church. When everyone dies to self and exalts Jesus, denominational divisions and theological debates fade away as everyone looks to the throne and lives Throne Life. F.J. Huegel expresses this vision: "The rising tide of divine life, once it rises high enough (it is forever overflowing all of its banks) . . . simply wipes out the great ecclesiastical barriers; the mighty walls of sects disappear." [277] He calls it "a deep oneness." This was Paul's desire, that we all come into the unity of the faith and the full knowledge of Christ (Eph 4:13).

Satisfied Yet Thirsty for More

Lays Potato Chips once had an advertising slogan that proclaimed "You can't eat just one." It was so good, you wanted more. You were satisfied, but with an unsatisfied satisfaction. That is what God desires for us—that we desire Him, yet want Him more. In the 1940s, A.W. Tozer published his classic book *The Pursuit of God*, calling people to this highest life:

> In this hour of all-but-universal darkness one cheering gleam appears: within the fold of conservative Christianity there are to be found increasing numbers of persons whose religious lives are marked by a growing hunger after God Himself. They are eager for spiritual realities and will not be put off with words, nor will they be content with correct "interpretations" of truth. They are athirst for God, and they will not be satisfied till they have drunk deep at the Fountain of Living Water.[278]

His call to hunger after God is just as timely and timeless today. *Come Up Higher!* has been about hungering after God Himself. It has been my prayer, along with Tozer, that you have become eager for spiritual realities and that you will not be content with less than all God has for you. Join with what Tozer called "The Fellowship of the Burning Heart." Pray with Tozer this prayer for more:

> O God, I have tasted Thy goodness, and it has both satisfied me and made me thirsty for more. I am painfully conscious of my need of further grace. I am ashamed of my lack of desire. O God, the Triune God, I want to want Thee; I long to be filled with longing; I thirst to be made more thirsty still. Show me Thy glory, I pray Thee, that so I may know Thee indeed. Begin in mercy a new work of love within me. Say to my soul, 'Rise up, my love, my fair one, and come away.' Then give me grace to rise and follow Thee up from this misty lowland where I have wandered so long. In Jesus' name, Amen.[279]

Where Jesus Is, 'Tis Heaven There

By Charles J. Butler

Since Christ my soul from sin set free,
This world has been a heaven to me;
Amid earth's sorrows and its woe,
Tis heaven my Jesus here to know
Once heaven seemed a far-off place
Till Jesus showed His smiling face;
Now it's begun within my soul,
T'will last while endless ages roll.
Oh, Hallelujah, yes, tis heaven!
Tis heaven to know my sins forgiven;
On land or sea, what matter where?
Where Jesus is, tis heaven there.

ENDNOTES

[1] George B. Peck, *Throne Life, or The Highest Christian Life* (Boston: Watchword Publishing Co., 1888), 171, 174-175, 177. Succeeding references come from this source.

[2] Andrew Murray, *The Holiest of All* (New York: Anson D. F. Randolph and Co., [1896], public domain. Succeeding references come from this source.

[3] Jessie Penn-Lewis, *The Warfare with Satan* (Dorset, Eng.: Overcomer Literature Trust, 1963), 63.

[4] Hannah Whitall Smith, *The Christian's Secret of a Happy Life* (Old Tappan, NJ: Fleming H. Revell Co., 1942), 168.

[5] Thomas Watson, *A Christian on Earth, Still in Heaven*, public domain, accessed online at http://www.gracegems.org/Watson/Christian on earth.htm. Succeeding references to Thomas Watson come from this source.

[6] Paraphrased in updated English from F.B. Meyer, *The Secret of Guidance* (Chicago: Moody Press, n.d.), 101-102.

[7] Sarah Foulkes Moore, *Our Throne Rights* (Los Angeles: Free Tract Society, n.d.), accessed online at http://img.sermonindex.net/modules/articles/article pdf.php?aid=28236. Succeeding references to Sarah Foulkes Moore come from this source.

[8] F.J. Huegel, *Bone of His Bone* (Grand Rapids: Zondervan, 1972), 91.

[9] Thomas Traherne, *Centuries of Meditations*, accessed online at http://www.ccel.org/ccel/traherne/centuries.html. Succeeding references to Traherne come from this source.

[10] T. Austin Sparks, "Captivity in the Lord," accessed online at http://www.sermonindex.net/modules/articles/index.php?view=article&aid=1403

[11] Francois Fenelon, *The Seeking Heart* (Sargent, GA: The SeedSowers, 1997), 29.

[12] Charles Spurgeon, *Morning by Morning* (Old Tappan, NJ: Fleming H. Revell, 1984), Nov. 23.

[13] Amy Carmichael, *Thou Givest . . . They Gather* (Fort Washington, PA: CLC, 1958), 9.

[14] Smith, *The Christian's Secret*, 160-161.

[15] Herbert Lockyer, *All The Messianic Prophecies Of The Bible* (Grand Rapids: Zondervan, 1973), 353.

[16] A.B. Simpson, *Christ in the Bible* (Camp Hill, PA: Christian Publications, 1992), 2:65.

[17] Penn-Lewis, *The Warfare with Satan*, 63.

[18] Penn-Lewis, *The Warfare with Satan*, 92.

[19] Lockyer, 353-354.

[20] Lockyer, 353-354.

[21] Lockyer, 354.

[22] Lockyer, 354.

[23] Lockyer, 359.

[24] Dave Browning, Glory Alleluia Music, 1986, CCLI #19272.

[25] A.W. Tozer, *The Knowledge of the Holy* (New York: Harper, 1961), 37.

[26] A.B. Simpson, *The Self Life or the Christ Life*, public domain.

[27] Neil T. Anderson, *Living Free in Christ* (Ventura, CA: Regal, 2000), 248.

[28] Simpson, *Christ in the Bible* (1992), 5:413-414.

[29] Watchman Nee, *Sit, Walk, Stand* (Ft. Washington, PA: CLC, 1957, 1971), 11-13, 22.

[30] J. Furman Miller, "Behold, Your Foes," *The Alliance Weekly*, Jan. 14, 1953, 6.

[31] Teresa of Avila, *Interior Castle*, Seventh Mansion, Chapter 2:15.

[32] John A. MacMillan, "Throne Worthiness," *The Alliance Weekly*, Sept. 7, 1946, 562.

[33] Thomas Brooks, "Choice Selections," *Heaven on Earth*, accessed http://www.gracegems.org/Brooks/heaven_on_earth_QUOTES.htm. Succeeding references to Brooks come from this source.

[34] Huegel, *Bone of His Bone*, 94-95.

[35] A.B. Simpson, "Resurrected and Seated in the Heavenlies," *The Christian and Missionary Alliance Weekly*, April 6, 1898, 318.

[36] Andrew Murray, *Abide in Christ* (Springdale, PA: Whitaker House, 1979), 70, 72.

[37] A.W. Tozer, *That Incredible Christian* (Harrisburg, PA: Christian Publications, 1964), 11-12.

Endnotes

38 Paul Billheimer, *Destined for the Throne* (Fort Washington, PA: CLC, 1975), 16.

39 Billheimer, 59, 89.

40 Murray, *Abide in Christ*, 59.

41 A.W. Tozer, *The Knowledge of the Holy* (New York: Harper and Row, 1961), 67.

42 Simpson, *In the School of Faith* (New York: Christian Alliance Publishing Co., 1894), 25-26.

43 Simpson, *Christ in the Bible* (1992), 2:319.

44 Charles Spurgeon, *Faith's Checkbook* (Chicago: Moody Press, n.d.), 4.

45 John A. MacMillan, *The Authority of the Believer* (Harrisburg, PA: Christian Publications, 1980), 49, 55.

46 Andrew Murray, *The Blood of the Cross* (Springdale, PA: Whitaker House, 1981), 132, 134.

47 Andrew Murray, *With Christ in the School of Prayer* (New York: Anson D.F. Randolph and Co., [1886]), 192.

48 Hannah Whitall Smith, *Living Confidently in God's Love* (Springdale, PA: Whitaker, 1984), 145-146.

49 George D. Watson, *Bridehood Saints* (Cincinnati: God's Revivalist, n.d.), 117-118, 120-122.

50 Oswald Chambers, *The Place of Help* (United Kingdom: Marshall Morgan & Scott, 1935), 101.

51 William Gurnall, *The Christian in Complete Armour*, ed. James S. Bell, Jr. (Chicago: Moody Press, 1994), August 27.

52 Andrew Murray, *The Two Covenants* (Fort Washington, PA: Christian Literature Crusade, 1974), 74.

53 A.J. Gordon, cited in Mrs. Charles Cowman, *Streams in the Desert*, Vol. 1 (Grand Rapids: Zondervan, [1925] 1972), Jan. 3.

54 Smith, *The Christian's Secret*, 166-167.

55 Adapted from K Neill Foster with Paul L. King, *Binding and Loosing: Exercising Authority over the Dark Powers* (Camp Hill, PA: Christian Publications, 1998), 115.

56 Murray, *With Christ in the School of Prayer*, 142.

57 Murray, *With Christ in the School of Prayer*, 136; see also 116-117, 178.

58 Adapted from Foster and King, *Binding and Loosing*, 115.

59 Oswald Chambers, *The Philosophy of Sin* (United Kingdom: Marshall Morgan & Scott, 1937), CD-ROM.

60 Meyer, *The Secret of Guidance*, 47.

61 Gurnall, *The Christian in Complete Armour*, August 7, February 18.

62 F.B. Meyer, *Five Musts of the Christian Life* (Chicago: Moody Press, 1927), 27-28.

63 Billheimer, 46-47.

64 A.B. Simpson, "Spiritual Talismans," *The Alliance Weekly*, June 14, 1919, 178.

65 Billheimer, 52.

66 MacMillan, *The Authority of the Believer*, 8.

67 John A. MacMillan, "Heavenly Quickening," *The Alliance Weekly*, Sept. 21, 1946, 594.

68 Meyer, *Five Musts of the Christian Life*, 27-28.

69 Much of this section is adapted from Paul L. King, *A Believer with Authority: The Life and Message of John A. MacMillan* (Camp Hill, PA: Christian Publications, 2001), and from Paul L. King, *Only Believe: Examining the Origin and Development of Classic and Contemporary Word of Faith Theologies* (Tulsa, OK: Word & Spirit Press, 2007). For footnotes and bibliographic information, consult these two books.

70 Meyer, *Five Musts of the Christian Life*, 65.

71 A.B. Simpson, *Christ in the Bible: Luke* (Harrisburg, PA: Christian Publications, n.d.), Vol. XIVB, 183.

72 A.T. Pierson, *The Acts of the Holy Spirit* (Harrisburg, PA: Christian Publications, 1980), 92.

73 A.B. Simpson, "The Authority of Faith," *The Alliance Weekly*, Apr. 23, 1938, 263.

74 John MacMillan, "Cleansed Within," *The Alliance Weekly*, Jan. 14, 1939, 19.

75 MacMillan, *The Authority of the Believer*, 57.

76 Paraphrased in updated English, Meyer, *The Secret of Guidance*, 102.

77 Nee, *Sit, Walk, Stand*, 63.

78   A.W. Tozer, *The Pursuit of God* (Camp Hill, PA: Christian Publications, 1982, 1993), 34.

79   A. W. Tozer, *Born After Midnight* (Harrisburg, PA: Christian Publications Inc., 1959), 94-95.

80   A.B. Simpson, Editorial, *The Alliance Weekly*, Oct. 27, 1906, 257.

81   A.B. Simpson, *Christ in the Bible: Matthew* (Harrisburg, PA: Christian Publications, n.d.), Vol. XIII, 163.

82   A.W. Tozer, *Wingspread* (Harrisburg, PA: Christian Publications, 1943), 79.

83   L.H. Ziemer, *The Story of My Conversion and Relative Experiences* (Toledo, OH: Toledo Gospel Tabernacle, n.d.), 23.

84   Mary Mullen, "A New Experience," *The Christian and Missionary Alliance Weekly*, Oct. 5, 1907, 17.

85   Dr. Thomas Moseley, "Revival at Nyack," *The Alliance Weekly*, Oct. 10, 1942, 643.

86   A.W. Tozer, *Worship: The Missing Jewel* (Camp Hill, PA: Christian Publications, 1992), 20-21.

87   Simpson, *Christ in the Bible* (1992), 2:319.

88   Howard Taylor, *Hudson Taylor's Spiritual Secret* (Chicago: Moody Press, 1932), 157.

89   Oswald Chambers, *Still Higher for His Highest* (Grand Rapids: Zondervan, 1970), 20.

90   A.B. Simpson, *The Self Life or the Christ Life*, public domain.

91   Chrysostom, Homilies on Ephesians, Homily 3.

92   Robert J. Stamps, "God and Man at Table Are Sat Down," c. 1975.

93   Thomas Brooks, "Choice Selections," *Heaven on Earth*, accessed http://www.gracegems.org/Brooks/heaven_on_earth_QUOTES.htm

94   Thomas Watson, *The Lord's Supper*, accessed online at http://www.gracegems.org/Watson/Lords%20Supper.htm. References from Watson in this chapter come from this source.

95   Paul Brand and Philip Yancey, *In His Image* (Grand Rapids: Zondervan, 1984), 104.

96   Brand, 95.

97   Brand, 102-103.

[98] A.B. Simpson, "The Significance of the Lord's Supper," *C&MA Weekly*, May 18, 1901, 270.

[99] A.W. Tozer, *Worship: The Missing Jewel* (Camp Hill, PA: Christian Publications, 1992), 20-21.

[100] Lloyd John Oglivie, *The Cup of Wonder: Communion Meditations* (Grand Rapids: Baker, 1976, 1985), 14-15.

[101] Oglivie, 15.

[102] Simpson, "The Significance of the Lord's Supper," 270.

[103] A.B. Simpson, "Power," *The Alliance Weekly*, Dec. 27, 1913, 195.

[104] Chrysostom, cited in *Ancient Christian Commentary on Scripture: New Testament, Ia: Matthew 1-13*, ed. Manlio Simonetti (Downers Grove, IL: IVP, 2001), 126.

[105] John A. MacMillan, "Reverence for God," *The Alliance Weekly*, Nov. 26, 1938, 755.

[106] Murray, *Abide in Christ*, 139.

[107] John A. MacMillan, "A Revival of Prayer," *The Alliance Weekly*, Nov. 12, 1938, 722.

[108] John A. MacMillan, "The Authority of the Intercessor," *The Alliance Weekly*, May 23, 1936, 334.

[109] MacMillan, "The Authority of the Intercessor," 334.

[110] MacMillan, *The Authority of the Believer*, 93, 96.

[111] MacMillan, *The Authority of the Believer*, 49, 55.

[112] Charles Spurgeon, "True Prayer, True Power," *The New Park Street Pulpit* (Grand Rapids: Zondervan, 1964), 6:337.

[113] Charles Spurgeon, *The Power of Prayer in a Believer's Life*, Robert Hall, comp. and ed. (Lynnwood, WA: Emerald Books, 1993), 27.

[114] Simpson, *A Larger Christian Life* (Harrisburg, PA: Christian Publications, n.d.), 11.

[115] A.B. Simpson, *The Life of Prayer* (Camp Hill, PA: Christian Publications, 1989), 60.

[116] Charles H. Spurgeon, "Golden Key of Prayer," Sermon #619, *The Metropolitan Tabernacle Pulpit*, Vol. 11 (1865), 152, updated language.

[117] A.T. Pierson, *The New Acts of the Apostles* (New York: Baker and Taylor, 1894), 193.

Endnotes

● ● ●

118 MacMillan, *The Authority of the Believer*, 23.

119 Spurgeon, "True Prayer, True Power," 336.

120 Simpson, *Christ in the Bible* (1992), 3:498.

121 Simpson, *Christ in the Bible* (1992), 3:498.

122 E.M. Bounds, *Purpose in Prayer* (Chicago: Moody Press, n.d.), 24.

123 Bounds, *Purpose in Prayer*, 45.

124 A.T. Pierson, *Lessons in the School of Prayer* (Dixon, MO: Rare Christian Books, n.d.), 60-61.

125 Paraphrased from J. Furman Miller, "Breaking Up Our Breakdowns," *The Alliance Weekly*, Oct. 15, 1952, 664.

126 Miller, "Breaking Up Our Breakdowns," 664.

127 MacMillan, *The Authority of the Believer*, 36.

128 J. Furman Miller, "Behold, Your Foes," *The Alliance Weekly*, Jan. 14, 1953, 6.

129 Kris Vallotton, *Spirit Wars: Winning the Invisible Battle Against Sin and the Enemy* (Minneapolis: Chosen Books, 2012), 123.

130 Oswald Chambers, *Not Knowing Whither* (United Kingdom: Marshall Morgan & Scott, 1934), CD-ROM.

131 Oswald Chambers, *My Utmost for His Highest*, (New York: Dodd, Mead, and Co., [1935] 1963), June 27.

132 Chambers, *The Place of Help*, 100.

133 Nee, *Sit, Walk, Stand*, 23.

134 Nee, *Sit, Walk, Stand*, 27.

135 Oswald Chambers, *Studies in the Sermon on the Mount*, (United Kingdom: Marshall Morgan & Scott, 1929), CD-ROM.

136 Oswald Chambers, *Disciples Indeed* (United Kingdom: Marshall Morgan & Scott, 1955), CD-ROM.

137 May Mabette Anderson, "The Prayer of Faith: Part II," *C&MA Weekly*, Feb. 24, 1906, 106-107.

138 Murray, *The Two Covenants*, 74.

139 Chambers, *The Place of Help*, 94.

140 Chambers, *My Utmost for His Highest*, October 5.

141 Chambers, *The Place of Help*, 174.

142 Chambers, *My Utmost for His Highest*, March 27, CD-ROM.

143 Terry Law, *The Truth About Angels* (Lake Mary, FL: Creation House, 1994), 167.

144 John Paul Jackson, *Needless Casualties of War* (Sutton, NH: Streams Publications, 1999), 8.

145 Ruth Paxson, *Life on the Highest Plane*, accessed online at http://bartimaeus.us/pub_dom/lothp-v2.html

146 A.B. Simpson, *Wholly Sanctified* Public domain, accessed https://online.ambrose.edu/alliancestudies/simpson/wholsanc.html

147 Chambers, *My Utmost for His Highest*, May 29.

148 Edith Beyerle, "Daily Meditation," *The Alliance Weekly*, June 21, 1941, 399

149 A.B. Simpson, *The Four-Fold Gospel* (Harrisburg, PA: Christian Publications, n.d.), 39-40.

150 A.B. Simpson, *Present Truths or the Supernatural* (Harrisburg, PA: Christian Publications, reprint 1967), 65.

151 A.J. Gordon, *The Ministry of the Spirit* (Minneapolis: Bethany Fellowship, 1964), 116.

152 Oswald J Smith, *The Baptism with the Holy Spirit* (New York: Christian Alliance Publishing Co., 1925), 47.

153 Carrie Judd Montgomery, "A Year with the Comforter," *Confidence*, Nov. 15, 1909, 229.

154 Ira E. David, "Sunday School Lesson: The Gift of the Holy Spirit," *The Alliance Weekly*, June 20, 1931, 406, 408.

155 A.W. Tozer, *Tragedy in the Church, The Missing Gifts* (Harrisburg, PA: Christian Publications, 1978), 29, 30.

156 A.B. Simpson, "The Dynamite of God," *The Alliance Weekly*, Oct. 20, 1917, 36

157 Cited in Eunice Perkins, *Joybringer Bosworth* (Dayton, OH: John J. Scruby, 1921), 74.

158 A. B. Simpson, "Fire-Touched Lips," *C&MA Weekly*, Sept. 12, 1908, 404.

159 I. E. David, "The Gift of the Spirit," *The Alliance Weekly*, June 20, 1931, 406.

160 A.B. Simpson, Editorial, *Living Truths*, Apr. 1906, 198.

Endnotes

161 William C. Stevens, "Divine Healing in Relation to Revivals," *C&MA Weekly*, Feb. 28, 1903, 124.

162 Tozer, *Tragedy in the Church*, 33, 42.

163 Charles Spurgeon, *What the Holy Spirit Does in a Believer's Life* (Lynnwood, WA: Emerald Books, 1993), 14, 51-52.

164 A.B. Simpson, "How to Receive Divine Healing," *Word, Work, and World*, July-Aug., 1885, 203.

165 A.B. Simpson, cited by a reporter in "Healing by Faith: Sick Persons Miraculously Cured," Simpson Scrapbook, p. 200, C&MA Archives.

166 John A. MacMillan, "Love's Divine Overflow," *The Alliance Weekly*, May 18, 1940, 306.

167 Mary Gainforth, *The Life and Healing of Mrs. Mary Gainforth*, (Trenton, Ontario: Jarrett Printing and Publishing Co., [1924?]), 41.

168 Carrie Judd Montgomery, *Under His Wings* (Oakland, CA: Triumphs of Faith, 1936), 168-170.

169 T.J. McCrossan, *Bodily Healing and the Atonement* (Harrisburg: Christian Alliance Publishing Co., 1927), 111-112.

170 DeVern Fromke, *No Other Foundation* (Cloverdale, IN: Sure Foundation, 1965), 76.

171 In this chapter, I have not relied upon the testimonies and teaching of classical Pentecostals or modern charismatics, but rather of those in the classic holiness and higher life traditions, so that readers can see that this is not just the experience of Pentecostals. Most of the references to these quotes can be found in my books *Genuine Gold* and *Nuggets of Genuine Gold*.

172 A.W. Tozer, *The Purpose of Man* (Ventura, CA: Regal, 2009), 30.

173 McCrossan, *Speaking with Other Tongues* (Harrisburg, PA: Christian Publications, 1927), 4.

174 Simpson, *The Life of Prayer*, 60.

175 Quotes in this section are cited or adapted from Paul L. King, *Only Believe: Examining the Origin and Development of Classic and Contemporary Word of Faith Theologies* (Tulsa, OK: Word & Spirit Press, 2008).

176 Oswald Chambers, *Biblical Psychology* (Grand Rapids: Discovery House, 1962, 1995), 43.

177 Charles Spurgeon, *All of Grace* (Springdale, PA: Whitaker House, 1981, 1983), 45.

178 Carrie Judd Montgomery, *Secrets of Victory* (Oakland, CA: Triumphs of Faith, 1921), 28. Succeeding references to Carrie come from this public domain source unless otherwise noted.

179 Albert Hibbert, *Smith Wigglesworth—The Secret of His Power* (Tulsa, OK: Harrison House, 1993), 103.

180 Charles Price, *The Real Faith* (Pasadena, CA: Charles A. Price Publishing Company, 1940, 1968), 54.

181 E.M. Bounds, *The Complete Works of E.M. Bounds: Book 1: The Necessity of Prayer* (Grand Rapids: Baker, 1990), 38.

182 Chambers, *My Utmost for His Highest*, 81.

183 T.J. McCrossan, *Christ's Paralyzed Church X-Rayed* (Youngstown, OH: Rev. C.E. Humbard, 1937), 320-321.

184 Charles Spurgeon, *Spiritual Warfare in a Believer's Life* (Lynnwood, WA: Emerald Books, 1993), 156.

185 Cited in Paul L. King, *Only Believe: Examining the Origin and Development of Classic and Contemporary Word of Faith Theologies* (Tulsa, OK: Word & Spirit Press, 2008), 179-184.

186 Watchman Nee, *God's Plan and the Overcomers* (New York: Christian Fellowship Publishers, 1977), 75.

187 Bounds, *The Complete Works of E.M. Bounds: Book 1: The Necessity of Prayer*, 38.

188 Simpson, *The Life of Prayer*, 70.

189 Oswald Chambers, *Daily Thoughts for Disciples* (Grand Rapids: Discovery House, [1976] 1994), Apr. 20.

190 Spurgeon, *The Metropolitan Tabernacle Pulpit*, Vol. 24, 645.

191 J. Hudson Taylor, "Reckon on God's Faithfulness," *Triumphs of Faith*, July 1902, 159.

192 Chambers, *The Place of Help*, 160.

193 Nee, *God's Plan and the Overcomers*, 29.

194 Murray, *With Christ in the School of Prayer*, 52.

195 A.B. Simpson, *The Gospel of Healing* (Harrisburg, PA: Christian Publications, 1915), 88-89.

Endnotes

[196] Cowman, *Streams in the Desert*, July 7.

[197] Wigglesworth, *Faith That Prevails* (Springfield, MO: Gospel Publishing House, 1938), 18-19.

[198] R.A. Torrey, *The Power of Prayer and the Prayer of Power* (Grand Rapids: Zondervan, 1924), 140.

[199] MacMillan, *The Authority of the Believer*, 67-68.

[200] Simpson, *Christ in the Bible* (1992), 3:498.

[201] Pierson, *Lessons in the School of Prayer*, 59-60.

[202] E.M. Bounds, *Purpose in Prayer* (Chicago: Moody Press, n.d.), 24.

[203] MacMillan, *The Authority of the Believer*, 60.

[204] Spurgeon, "True Prayer, True Power," *The New Park Street Pulpit* (Grand Rapids: Zondervan, 1964), Vol. 6, 336.

[205] Pierson, *Lessons in the School of Prayer*, 60-61.

[206] Pierson, *Lessons in the School of Prayer*, 60-61.

[207] Spurgeon, "True Prayer, True Power," *The New Park Street Pulpit*, Vol. 6, 336.

[208] Pierson, *Lessons in the School of Prayer*, 59-60.

[209] Simpson, *CITB* (1992), 6:387.

[210] Simpson, *Days of Heaven on Earth* (Camp Hill, PA: Christian Publications, 1984), Oct. 6.

[211] Smith, *The Christian's Secret*, 32.

[212] Smith, *The Christian's Secret*, 36.

[213] Tozer, *Born After Midnight*, 106-107.

[214] Howard Taylor, *Hudson Taylor's Spiritual Secret*, 26.

[215] Steer, *Spiritual Secrets of George Müller*, 87.

[216] Simpson, *In the School of Faith*, 35.

[217] Simpson, *A Larger Christian Life*, 71.

[218] Chambers, *My Utmost for His Highest*, May 25.

[219] Simpson, *Days of Heaven on Earth*, Aug. 24.

[220] Simpson, *The Land of Promise* (Harrisburg, PA: Christian Publications, 1969), 34-35.

[221] Simpson, *In the School of Faith*, 52.

222   Amy Carmichael, *You Are My Hiding Place*, arranged by David Hazard (Minneapolis: Bethany House, 1991), 44.

223   Chambers, *Daily Thoughts for Disciples*, Nov. 7.

224   Friedrich Zuendel, *The Awakening* (Farmington, PA: Plough Publishing House, 1999), 139.

225   Smith Wigglesworth, *The Ever-Increasing Faith* (Springfield, MO: Gospel Publishing House, 1924), 11.

226   Carmichael, *Thou Givest . . . They Gather*, 110.

227   Bounds, *Book 2: The Essentials of Prayer*, from *The Complete Works of E.M. Bounds*, 2:114.

228   Hudson Taylor, *Union and Communion with Christ* (Minneapolis: Bethany House, n.d.), 42.

229   Simpson, *CITB*, (1992) 6:206.

230   Spurgeon, *Faith's Checkbook*, 5.

231   Spurgeon, *Faith's Checkbook*, 5.

232   Spurgeon, *Morning by Morning*, Oct. 26.

233   Simpson, *CITB* (1992), 1:392.

234   Hudson Taylor, *Union and Communion with Christ*, 20.

235   Spurgeon, *The Triumph of Faith in a Believer's Life*, 83.

236   Simpson, *Days of Heaven on Earth*, Oct. 6.

237   Amy Carmichael, cited in Elliot, *A Chance to Die* (Old Tappan: Revell, 1987), 189.

238   Elliot, 227.

239   A.W. Tozer, *That Incredible Christian*, 12.

240   Tozer, *The Pursuit of God*, 97.

241   George D. Watson, *Holiness Manual* (Boston: McDonald, Gill, & Co., 1882), 50-51.

242   Watson, *Holiness Manual*, 50-51.

243   Simpson, *Christ the Bible* (1992), 5:84.

244   Simpson, *A Larger Christian Life*, 13.

245   Thomas Watson, *The Christian on Earth, Still in Heaven.*

246   Simpson, *The Self Life or the Christ Life*. Public domain.

Endnotes

[247] Watchman Nee, *The Release of the Spirit* (Indianapolis, IN: Sure Foundation, 1965), 54.

[248] Keith M. Bailey, *Divine Healing: The Children's Bread* (Harrisburg, PA: Christian Publications, 1977), 10.

[249] Andrew Murray, *Divine Healing* (Springdale, PA: Whitaker House, 1982), 119.

[250] A.B. Simpson, *Triumphs of Faith*, Nov. 1922, 252.

[251] A.B. Simpson, *Danger Lines in the Deeper Life* (Camp Hill, PA: Christian Publications, 1991), 80.

[252] Lewis Drummond, *Spurgeon: Prince of Preachers* (Grand Rapids: Kregel, 1992), 221. Italics mine.

[253] Simpson, "Inquiries and Answers," *Word, Work and World*, Nov. 1886, 290-291. Italics mine.

[254] Simpson, *The Gospel of Healing*, 64.

[255] Simpson, *In the School of Faith*, 217-218.

[256] Simpson, *In the School of Faith*, 218-219.

[257] A.B. Simpson, *Christ for the Body* (Nyack, N.Y.: The Christian and Missionary Alliance, n.d.), n.p.

[258] Charles Spurgeon, *1000 Devotional Thoughts* (Grand Rapids: Baker, 1976), 470.

[259] Simpson, *Days of Heaven on Earth*, Apr. 8.

[260] S.D. Gordon, *The Healing Christ* (New York: Fleming H. Revell, 1924), 104, 108.

[261] S.D. Gordon, 62-63, 104, 108.

[262] Howard Taylor, *Hudson Taylor's Spiritual Secret*, 156.

[263] Carrie Judd, "Faith Rest Cottage," *Triumphs of Faith*, Apr. 1888, 96.

[264] Andrew Murray, cited in Howard Taylor, *Hudson Taylor's Spiritual Secret*, 236.

[265] Roger Steer, *Spiritual Secrets of George Müller* (Wheaton: Harold Shaw Publishers, 1985), 87.

[266] Fenelon, 9.

[267] Spurgeon, *Faith's Checkbook*, 87.

[268] Meyer, *The Secret of Guidance*, 27.

[269] Simpson, *Days of Heaven on Earth*, Apr. 8.

270 Oswald Chambers, *My Utmost for His Highest*, March 27.

271 Spurgeon, "Essential Points in Prayer," *The Power of Prayer*, 136-137.

272 Spurgeon, *The Power of Prayer*, 137.

273 A.W. Tozer, *The Root of the Righteous* (Harrisburg, PA: Christian Publications, 1955), 145-146.

274 Tozer, *The Root of the Righteous*, 146.

275 Tozer, *Man, the Dwelling Place of God* (Camp Hill, PA: Christian Publications, 1966), 174.

276 A.W. Tozer, *I Call It Heresy* (Camp Hill, PA: Christian Publications, 1991), 146-147.

277 Huegel, *Bone of His Bone*, 94.

278 Tozer, *The Pursuit of God*, 7.

279 Tozer, *The Pursuit of God*, 20.

ABOUT THE AUTHOR

Dr. Paul King, an ordained minister with The Christian and Missionary Alliance, served for 16 years on the faculty of Oral Roberts University as Director of Bible Institute Programs and as an adjunct professor of theology and ministry. He received the Doctor of Ministry from Oral Roberts University and Doctor of Theology from the University of South Africa. Author of ten books, he was awarded Scholar of the Year at Oral Roberts University in 2006, and served as Scholar-at-Large at Alliance Theological Seminary, and as an adjunct professor and consultant for Crown College.

Dr. King speaks in churches, conferences, and seminars interdenominationally and internationally, teaching on ministry and leadership development, the deeper and higher life in Christ, revival and the ministry of the Holy Spirit, spiritual discernment and spiritual warfare, women in ministry, elder training, and worship. He specializes in research on 19th and early 20th century movements of holiness, healing, faith, and the Holy Spirit. As a cancer overcomer, he teaches and ministers on divine healing. He consults with churches and educational institutions regarding church health and ministry and leadership training.

Dr. King and his wife Kathy married in 1975, and reside in Broken Arrow, Oklahoma, where he pastors a church plant, Higher Life Fellowship. They have two adult children, Sarah and Christopher. You can find more information about Paul King on his website www.paulkingministries.com.

OTHER TITLES BY PAUL L. KING

God's Healing Arsenal: A Divine Battle Plan for Overcoming Distress and Disease
A wide array of healing weapons God uses to bring healing and victory. Forged in the fires of the author's own personal battle overcoming cancer. "Nuggets from the whole spectrum of God's people. . . . sage advice"—Dr. Neil T. Anderson ISBN-10: 0882700111 ISBN-13: 978-0882700113 Paperback

Finding Your Niche: 12 Keys to Opening God's Doors for Your Life
Universal biblical principles from more than 35 years of ministry experience for unlocking the gateways to your assignment from God and encountering new vistas of God's purposes for your life and calling. Discussion and study questions included. ISBN 10: 0-9785352-8-6 ISBN 13: 978-0-9785352-8-5 Paperback

Moving Mountains: Lessons in Bold Faith from Great Evangelical Leaders
Amazing stories and teachings of bold, wise faith from George Müller, Hudson Taylor, Charles Spurgeon, Andrew Murray, A.B. Simpson, Hannah Whitall Smith, Oswald Chambers, E.M. Bounds, Amy Carmichael, A.W. Tozer, and more! Study guide included. *"Feast on wind and fire!"—Calvin Miller* ISBN 0-8007-9375-7 Paperback

A Believer with Authority: The Life and Message of John A. MacMillan
The ground-breaking biography and teachings of the Christian and Missionary Alliance missionary and professor who was a trail-blazing pioneer in spiritual warfare and the seminal writer on the authority of the believer. *Endorsed by Jack Hayford and Neil Anderson.* ISBN 0-87509-917-3 Paperback

Genuine Gold: The Cautiously Charismatic Story of the Early Christian and Missionary Alliance

The rediscovered and fully-documented history of the supernatural in the C&MA, featuring first-hand testimonies of early Alliance charismatic experiences (even before Azusa Street), relationships between the C&MA and the early Pentecostal movement, and evidences of historical drift and recovery. *"[A] valuable book. . . . King's research is impressive."—Pneuma: The Journal of the Society for Pentecostal Studies* ISBN 0-9785352-0-0 Paperback

Binding and Loosing: Exercising Authority over the Dark Powers (co-author K. Neill Foster)

Understanding properly the biblical and theological concept and sound practice of combating the powers that war against Christ and His Church through binding and loosing according to Matthew 16:19—when it is appropriate, when it works and when it does not. Illustrated from real life experiences. Study guide included. ISBN 0-87509-852-5 Paperback

Only Believe: Examining the Origin and Development of Classic and Contemporary Word of Faith Theologies

"The definitive, comprehensive study of the teachings and practices of faith throughout church history. Thoroughly documented with classic & contemporary citations, it breaks new ground, uncovers new historical & theological information about the origins of faith teaching & practice; corrects inaccurate information & misinterpretations; discerns healthy & unhealthy teachings and practices in today's Word of Faith movement; & provides sound counsel for walking by faith . . . at once scholarly, accessible, & practical."—Mark E. Roberts, Ph.D. ISBN 978-0-9785352-6-1 Paperback

Anointed Women: The Rich Heritage of Women in Ministry in The Christian and Missionary Alliance

The remarkable stories of women used by God in amazing ways, documenting hundreds of women who served as Alliance pastors, evangelists, and teachers, planted hundreds of churches, and led thousands of people to salvation in Christ, healing, and a deeper Christian life. ISBN 978-0-9819526-7-3 Paperback

Nuggets of Genuine Gold: Simpson, Tozer, Jaffray and Other Christian and Missionary Alliance Leaders on Experiencing the Spirit-Empowered Life

Quotes, testimonies, and experiences from Alliance leaders on the baptism in the Spirit, supernatural gifts and manifestations of the Spirit, Spirit-filled life and worship, spiritual discernment and warfare. ISBN 978-0-9819526-6-6 Paperback

To order copies see www.paulkingministries.com
or e-mail paulkingministries@gmail.com

www.ingramcontent.com/pod-product-compliance
Lightning Source LLC
Chambersburg PA
CBHW071416090426
42737CB00011B/1487